Triumph at the Cross

Lenten Devotions
for Repentance and Renewal

Harold L. Senkbeil

Northwestern Publishing House
Milwaukee, Wisconsin

Library of Congress Card 99-76205

Northwestern Publishing House
1250 N. 113th St., Milwaukee, WI 53226-3284
© 1999 by Northwestern Publishing House.
Published 1999
Printed in the United States of America
ISBN 0-8100-1214-6

Table of Contents

As We Set Out

The Christian church has, for centuries, practiced a 40-day fast preceding Easter, as a time for meditation, prayer—and renewal. The renewal comes not by way of self-denial, but by way of the gospel: the good news of sins forgiven and life restored through Christ our Lord. In his innocent suffering and death and by his holy, precious blood, he restores, renews, and cleanses broken hearts through faith in him.

In the pages that follow, you will find daily devotions to guide you on your Lenten journey of repentance and renewal in the gospel. Special thanks to Dr. Beverly Yahnke, whose editorial gifts shrunk full-length sermons into manageable readings for the 40 days of Lent. On the intervening Sundays, you are provided a history of the Savior's passion compiled from the four gospels. These 40 devotions, 6 Sunday passion narratives, plus a final Easter meditation are offered as companions on your path towards renewal. Blessed Lent!

—Rev. Harold L. Senkbeil, STM
Elm Grove Evangelical Lutheran Church
Elm Grove, Wisconsin
Reformation Day 1999

Where in the World Is God?

Ash Wednesday

*The word is very near you; it is in your mouth
and in your heart so you may obey it.*
(Deuteronomy 30:14)

A crucial question plagues the world today: "Where in the world is God?" The skeptics put it this way: "Where in the world *is* God, anyway?" For them the tragedies and perplexities of life are just too overwhelming. They can't make any sense out of it—how a God who is supposedly good and all powerful could allow such things to happen. In fact, they're not at all sure that there is a God.

But for those of us who are embarking on a Lenten journey this Ash Wednesday, it's not a question of the existence of God—it's simply a matter of where we can get in touch with God. The problems of life and the nagging burden of sin make this question an urgent one. We all need to know: "Where in the world is God? How can we contact him?"

There's nothing we human beings would rather do than climb up into heaven to get the straight scoop from God. But this arrogant idea that we can get in touch with God through our own power ignores the fact that there is a great barrier between God and man: the wall of sin built by man himself. That wall is so high and so strong that no human effort can penetrate it. That's why it's so laughable that people would even talk about coming to God under their own steam.

But, though we could not come to him, he has come to us. God, the creator of the whole universe, came down to planet earth. He came in lowly weakness, clothed in human skin and bones. And even though it meant death—even a horrible death on the cross—he humbled himself so that he could take all our guilt on himself and remove forever the barrier of sin.

This is the God we have. He comes into this world to rescue us. He shoulders his cross and carries our sin in his own sinless body and then ultimately dies our death. Remarkable, isn't it? This God of ours will stop at nothing to give us his love.

Where in the world is God? We have a God who comes down to meet us in the word of his gospel. Even to touch and handle the living flesh of Jesus is not beyond our reach, for he condescends to attach his word of promise to the earthly elements of bread and wine. And in that Word made visible, we have the sign and seal of our redemption and the encouragement to faith and hope and love. "For you," he says to every weary soul weighed down by sin and plagued by trial, "for the forgiveness of your sin." The real presence of Jesus in his Holy Supper is not some dry doctrine, but living reality. We have his Word on it.

Where in the world is God? Not far away. In the precious gospel of Jesus, his Son, he is in your mouth and in your heart, throughout this Lenten journey, and even into eternity.

Jesus, I will ponder now on your holy passion. With your Spirit me endow for such meditation. Grant that I in love and faith may the image cherish of your suffering, pain, and death that I may not perish. Amen.

His Will Was Done

"Father, if you are willing, take this cup from me;
yet not my will, but yours be done."
(Luke 22:42)

For six weeks God's people ponder and meditate upon the suffering of our Lord. Some consider this unrelenting look at the cross and the suffering of Jesus a little gruesome or gory. Others look upon it much as they would view a baseball game with no hits or a concert with no favorite tunes. Lent tends to drag a bit, so much so, that by the end of Lent when they hear Jesus announce, "It is finished," they breathe a little sigh of relief and say, "Thank God, it's over."

It's amazing how many Lenten seasons we can live through and listen to Jesus—and still not really hear him. We watch and we pray all through Lent, but sometimes we tend to view the whole thing as an awesome saga on a grand scale—a kind of monumental performance, like watching the passion play or hearing Handel's *Messiah*. It's a moving time and a moving experience. But when we get to the last act, we simply go back home again as if nothing happened. It's as though all that Jesus endured is just a story on a big screen, with a great cast and a wonderful screenplay, but, nonetheless, just a story.

It's nice while it lasts. It tugs at our heartstrings and overwhelms us with its scope and passion. But when it's all over, we put on our coats and go back home to reality. And the reality back home isn't always very nice. For there are the same tensions and struggles, the same bottomless cravings and temptations, the same sad record of sin and sorrow, the same old hurts and wounds.

We live, not just with an "abstract" thing called sin, but with all the *concrete fallout* of that sin in terms of fractured and broken lives and torn and wounded consciences. No matter how nice and quiet and serene we appear on the outside, on the inside we are tattered and torn, frazzled and worn. We ache for recovery and renewal and healing and peace of heart and mind and soul.

And that's what brings us to walk the Lenten pathway once again. That's what invites us to rehearse yet one more time the astonishing plan of God for our salvation. That's what compels us to follow Jesus to Calvary—where he hung naked and despised before the mocking eyes of his enemies—where he suffered and died for the sins of the world.

This was the ordeal Jesus dreaded—the cup of wrath he pleaded not to drink. "Yet not my will," Jesus had prayed to his Father, "but yours be done." And at the cross, God himself—for Jesus is God—endured our pain in order that we might have his healing. He made the complete payment for all our sins, once and for all. God's will was done.

And all that Jesus earned by his cross and suffering, he now extends to you and me in his holy gospel and precious sacraments. He comes to meet us in his Holy Word and Sacrament—to lift our burdens, to carry our sorrows, to erase our guilt. He comes to bring us joy instead of sorrow, peace instead of anxiety, and the very life of Christ himself instead of the death in which we live.

A Lamb goes uncomplaining forth, our guilt and evil bearing. And, laden with the sins of earth, none else the burden sharing. Goes patient on, grows weak and faint, to slaughter led without complaint, that spotless life to offer, bears shame and stripes and wounds and death, anguish and mockery and says, "Willing all this I suffer." Amen.

Self-Denial

And Jesus answered them, "The hour has come
for the Son of man to be glorified. Truly, truly, I say to
you, unless a grain of wheat falls into the earth and dies,
it remains alone; but if it dies, it bears much fruit.
He who loves his life loses it, and he who hates his life
in this world will keep it for eternal life."
(John 12:23-25 RSV)

It's comparatively easy to "give up something for Lent." Movies or parties or even liquor and chocolate, we can forgo for a season. And it might even be a good thing for us to do that once in a while as a spiritual exercise. But Jesus invites us to something far more radical. He doesn't ask us to deny *something* to ourselves. He asks us to deny *ourselves*.

To our ears, tuned to the vibrations of the world we live in, the word *self-denial* has a discordant ring to it. "We need to *assert* ourselves, not *deny* ourselves," our culture says, "to build ourselves up, not tear ourselves down." Self-esteem is as American as apple pie. It's one of our essential rights. That's the way *we* think.

But Jesus will have none of it. Not because he wants to hurt us, but because he wants to heal us. His words might sound like a foreign language to us because we have been brainwashed by the culture around us. But in reality these words of Jesus are our mother tongue: "He who loves his life loses it, and he who hates his life in this world will keep it for eternal life."

Why would Jesus say such a thing? Because he loves us. Because he wants us to have life in all of its abundance, and not merely the cheap imitation stuff we think is life—but is really death in disguise. Because he wants us to give up slavery to sin and enjoy the glorious freedom of the children of God. Because he wants to loose us from the bondage of our sin, which is taking us to death, and to make us free through faith in him.

It's high time that we turn from slavery to freedom. It's high time to face facts. It's high time to recognize that within us there dwells no good thing, that is, in our sinful nature. In this holy season, we learn anew the cleansing and renewal that comes with repentance as we lay down the sin, deny the self, and take up the life we've already been given through Jesus Christ. That life belongs to all the baptized children of God—being buried into his death and raised with him by faith in the workings of God, who raised him from the dead. And the same God and Father who raised Christ Jesus will give life to our mortal bodies also by his Holy Spirit at work among us.

No wonder, then, that during Lent, we pray that our loving Father would create a clean heart and renew a right spirit within us, that he would not cast us away from his presence or take his Holy Spirit from us. And you can count on our heavenly Father to do all that for us, for Jesus' sake.

Grant that I your passion view with repentant grieving. Let me not bring shame to you by unholy living. How could I refuse to shun every sinful pleasure since for me God's only Son suffered without measure? Amen.

Where Is the Lamb?

*The next day John saw Jesus coming toward him
and said, "Look, the Lamb of God,
who takes away the sin of the world!"*
(John 1:29)

Every culture, even the most pagan and godless, has always tried to find some way to atone for sin. Human beings—whether their gods were the sun, moon, and stars or were fashioned from wood and stone—have always tried to make up for their guilt. Call it superstition if you want, but really it's mankind crying out, "Where's the way out? Where is the Lamb?"

Our modern gods are more sophisticated. Their names are often spelled with dollar signs and decorated with designer labels and advertised on glossy paper in print and in glitzy spots on TV. But behind this endless quest for more, our culture longs for God. It's as if we need to scream "Where is the Lamb?" but can only mumble, "What can I buy?"

And so our world goes whirling on its merry-go-round in pursuit of ultimate pleasure, anything to make us feel good and forget our pain or to help us ignore the pain of others. And that's what it's all about, don't you see? This mad rush of this world of ours to get things and to make people feel good is nothing new. Behind it all stands the same old question: "Where is the Lamb?" Where is the way out?

The answer is found near the Jordan River where John the Baptist lifts his arm, points a strong finger at the man from Nazareth, and resolves the question of all ages: "Look, the Lamb." This lamb—one of us, made under the law, hands still calloused from carpenter's tools, yet eyes burning bright with divine destiny—this lamb will be the final and complete sacrifice to atone for all sins. He is *the* lamb, "the Lamb of God, who takes away the sin of the world!"

And that means you no longer need to wonder what to do about the hole in your soul or the pain in your life or the guilt of your past. It means you don't have to keep trying to go it on your own, trying to deal with your own fears, sorrow, and shame. For Jesus is the Lamb of God. And he does take away the sin of the world. And when he takes it away, it's gone, all gone—erased forever in his blood, shed once and for all on his cross.

"Look!" John pointed to Jesus. But we can too. Though his flesh and blood are not visible to our eyes, still he is just as much with us as he was with John. Our bodies are washed in his Baptism; his Word is audible to our ears; his Supper is edible by mouth. In that washing, Word, and Supper comes Jesus himself, bringing the forgiveness of your sins, and his life and salvation, all of which he hands over to you. He came for you. He lived for you. He died for you. Now he comes again for you: "Look, the Lamb of God, who takes away the sin of the world!"

> Behold the Lamb of God for guilty sinners slain. Let it not be in vain that you have died! You for my Savior let me take; my only refuge let me make your pierced side. Amen.

The Word of God

The Passion of Our Lord Jesus Christ
Drawn from the Four Gospels

First Sunday in Lent

The Passover and the Lord's Supper

Now the Feast of Unleavened Bread, called the Passover, was approaching. Jesus said to his disciples, "As you know, the Passover festival will begin two days from now, and the Son of Man will be handed over to be crucified."

Then the chief priests and members of the Sanhedrin, the Jewish high council, gathered in the palace of Caiaphas the high priest. They were trying to find some reason for which they could arrest Jesus and kill him. They talked about setting up some kind of situation where they might trick or trap him into making a mistake. "But we mustn't do it during the Feast," they said. "We don't want to start a riot among the people."

Then Satan entered into the heart of Judas, called Iscariot, one of the Twelve. He went to the chief priests and the officers of the temple police and discussed with them how he might betray Jesus to them. Judas asked, "What will you give me to betray him to you?" They

19

counted out 30 silver coins and gave them to him. From that time on Judas began to look for an opportunity when Jesus was not surrounded by friendly crowds—a time when his enemies would have a good chance to arrest him.

On Thursday, the first day of the Feast of Unleavened Bread, when it was customary to sacrifice the Passover lamb, Jesus told Peter and John, "Go and get things ready for us to eat the Passover."

"Where do you want us to prepare it?" they asked.

Jesus replied, "Go into the city. You will meet a man carrying a jar of water. Follow him and he'll lead you to the right house. Tell the owner of the house, 'Our Teacher sends you this message: The time God has set for me is almost here. My disciples and I are going to celebrate the Passover at your house. Where is the room where we can eat the Passover meal?' He will show you a large upstairs room. It will be all set up and have everything we'll need. Prepare the feast for us there."

So the two of them went off to Jerusalem, where they found everything just as Jesus had said they would, and they got the Passover supper ready.

Later the same day, towards the end of the afternoon, Jesus and his disciples went to that house in Jerusalem. When it was time to eat, they took their places at the table, and Jesus said to them, "I can't tell you how much I have looked forward to eating this Passover supper with you before I die. For this is my last Passover. I will not eat another one until it finds fulfillment in the kingdom of God."

And while they were eating, Jesus took some bread and gave thanks. Then he broke the bread into pieces and gave them to his disciples, and said, "Take and eat: this is my body which is given for you; do this in remembrance of me."

In the same way, he also took a cup of wine. When he had said a prayer of thanksgiving, he gave it to them and said, "Drink of it, all of you. This cup is the new covenant in my blood, which is poured out for you and for many for the forgiveness of sins. Do this, whenever you drink it, in remembrance of me." They all drank from it.

Shortly after that the disciples began to argue among themselves as to which of them should be considered the greatest or most important disciple. So Jesus said to them, "The kings of this world treat their people like slaves; and those who exercise complete power over their people like to be looked upon as 'friends of the people.' But you are not to be like that. Instead, the greatest among you must act as if he's the least important person, and the one who is the leader must act like a servant. For who is greater? The one who is being served at the table or the one who serves him? Isn't it the one who sits at the table and has someone else waiting on him? And yet I am among you as one who serves, a servant. Now you are the ones who have stood faithfully by me through all my troubles and trials. And just as my Father has given me the right to rule, so I give you the same right, for you will eat and drink at my table in my kingdom, and you will sit on thrones, ruling over the 12 tribes of Israel."

Now Jesus knew that the time had come for him to leave this world and to go back to his Father. Having loved his own who are in the world, he loved them to the end. Jesus knew that the Father had put everything into his hands, and that he had come from God and was going back to God. He got up from the meal, took off his robe, and tied a towel around his waist. Then he poured water into a basin and began to wash the feet of his disciples and to dry them with the towel.

Jesus went from one disciple to another, washing their feet. When he came to Peter, Peter asked incredulously, "Lord, are you going to wash my feet?"

Jesus replied, "Right now, you don't realize what I'm doing, but some day you will."

"No," Peter protested, "you'll never wash my feet."

Jesus answered, "Unless I wash you, you can't belong to me."

"Then, Lord," Peter replied, "don't just wash my feet. Wash my hands and head too."

Jesus answered, "That won't be necessary. When a person has already taken a bath, he only needs to wash his feet to be clean all over. And you men are clean— all except one." Jesus meant Judas, for he knew who was going to betray him. That's why he said that not everyone was clean.

So after Jesus had washed his disciples' feet, he put his robe back on and took his place at the table again. "Do you know what I have done to you?" he asked. "You men call me 'Master' and 'Lord,' and it's right for you to do so, because that's what I am. I am your Lord and your Master—and yet I have just washed your feet. Now, since I have done this to you, you should wash one another's feet. I have given you this example that you should keep on doing what I have done for you. I tell you the truth, no servant is more important than his master, nor is a messenger greater than the one who sent him. Now that you know this truth, how happy you will be when you put it into practice.

"I'm not talking about all of you; I know whom I have chosen. There is an Old Testament prophecy that says: 'He who sits down to eat with me and shares my bread as my best friend will lift up his heel against me and betray me.' One of you is going to make this prophecy come true. I am telling you this now before it happens, so that when it does happen, you will believe that I am he.

"I tell you the truth, whoever receives anyone I send receives me; and whoever receives me receives the one who sent me."

Then Jesus became very sad and troubled. "Oh believe me, believe me," he said. "One of you is going to betray me."

The disciples were shocked. They stared at each other, wondering which of them could possibly do such a thing. One by one they began to ask, "Lord, is it I?"

Finally, Simon Peter motioned to John, who was sitting next to Jesus, that he should ask Jesus whom he meant.

John moved over closer to Jesus and whispered, "Lord, who is it?"

Quietly Jesus answered him, "It is the man to whom I will give this piece of bread after I've dipped it into the bowl of sauce. The Son of Man is going to suffer and die just as the Scriptures say he will. But woe to that man by whom the Son of Man is betrayed. It would be better for that man if he had never been born."

And when he had dipped the piece of bread, he handed it to Judas Iscariot.

Then Judas, who had already resolved to betray Jesus, said to him, "Master, am I the one?"

Jesus whispered, "You certainly are."

After Judas took the bread, Satan entered into his heart so that he would not give up his wicked plan to betray Jesus. And so Jesus said to him, "What you are about to do, do quickly." Judas got up from the table abruptly and strode out of the room. By now it was dark outside.

None of the disciples knew why Jesus had done what he did or why Judas left so quickly. But since he was the treasurer for Jesus and the disciples, some thought that Jesus was sending him out to buy something that was needed for the supper or, perhaps, that he was going out to give a gift to the poor.

After Judas was gone, Jesus said, "Now the Son of Man will receive glory and honor and will bring glory and honor to God by what he does. He will cause people to see how wonderful God is. If God is glorified in him, then God will glorify the Son in himself and will glorify him at once.

"My little children, I will not be with you very much longer. You're going to be looking for me, but just as I told the Jewish leaders, so I tell you now: Where I am going, you cannot come. A new commandment I give you: Love one another. You must love one another in the same way that I have loved you. And if you have this sort of love for one another, then all men will know that you are my disciples."

Simon Peter asked him, "Lord, where are you going?"

Jesus replied, "Where I'm going, you cannot follow now, but afterwards you will."

Peter asked, "Lord, why can't I follow you now? I will lay down my life for you."

Then Jesus answered, "Will you really lay down your life for me? Simon, Simon, Satan has asked to put you to the test, to sift you as wheat. But I have prayed for you that when Satan puts you through this terrible struggle, you will not lose your faith. And when you have repented of your sin and returned to me, you must go and strengthen your brothers, your fellow disciples, against Satan's temptations."

The Death That Heals

"Come, let us return to the LORD.
He has torn us to pieces but he will heal us;
he has injured us but he will bind up our wounds."
(Hosea 6:1)

There is a certain morbid fascination these days with tragedy and the macabre. Live video footage of people's personal calamities is passed off as entertainment. That's show business, I guess, in someone's twisted mentality.

But Lent is not a time for morbid fascination. We don't set aside these weeks of meditation to be entertained by gruesome gore or to be fascinated with the grotesque. Rather, we come to repent, to be renewed, and to be healed. And as we do so, we discover, all over again, that there is healing in Jesus Christ. It's just that his healing comes with a very high price tag. Christ's healing comes through death.

But that was all part of God's plan, you see. The sweeter part of the plan was the cuddly little baby in Bethlehem's manger, lying cozily among the animals.

But God's plan also required Jesus to be betrayed, beaten, and executed in bitter agony on his cross. Isaiah made that point absolutely clear many years before when he wrote, "It was the LORD's will to crush him" (Isaiah 53:10). So God made no mistake here. This is no glitch in the cosmic plan.

Nor is the annual observance of Lent an effort to muster up some sympathy for Jesus. He has no need for our sympathy. Any "poor Jesus" sentiments are entirely out of place. For he is not some helpless victim. No, he is the man in charge. And what he did, he did for us and for our salvation—and he did it willingly. He became our great High Priest—that he might offer the perfect sacrifice for sin and be raised again on the third day, never to die again. And we remember that it was the will of the Lord to crush him. As Hosea reminds us, "He has torn us to pieces but he will heal us; he has injured us but he will bind up our wounds."

If you have need for healing, if you've ever been injured deeply in heart and soul, you are not alone. I don't know your pain, your private fears, your particular worry and affliction. But Jesus does. He is a man of sorrows, well acquainted with grief. He knows your pain; after all, he bore it all within his very body.

So, if life has begun to get you down, if life has become a burden, if you've been worrying about the anxieties and stresses of life, worry no more. For along with the burden comes strength, and along with the sorrow comes relief. So we do not lose heart. We are washed and cleansed to be his own dear children, and he reaches down to strengthen us in his Holy Word and Sacrament. We know that the One who once was slain now lives eternally to save, to grant eternal life to all his own. And so we have hope this day, and every day, for all our days.

> **The will of God is always best and shall be done forever. And they who trust in him are blest; he will forsake them never. He helps indeed in time of need; he chastens with forbearing. They who depend on God, their friend, shall not be left despairing. Amen.**

Sin and Salvation

But he was pierced for our transgressions,
he was crushed for our iniquities;
the punishment that brought us peace was upon him,
and by his wounds we are healed.
(Isaiah 53:5)

As we go through life, you and I develop a lot of calluses on our souls. We get so used to sin that it doesn't seem to bother us all that much. We begin to play the same games as everyone else: the "cover up and pretend" game and the "everybody's doing it" game. No matter what the name of the game is, the bottom line is always the same: we brainwash ourselves into thinking that sin isn't all that bad, that it's no big deal.

God thinks otherwise. "The soul that sins shall die," he decrees. And if there is any doubt about how seriously God takes sin, consider Calvary. Take a good look this Lenten season, and there you will see what sin really looks like: the holy sinless God, wrapped in human flesh, hung up to die a painful, naked death in humiliation and shame. That's what sin looks like.

Sin isn't so bad, you would still argue? Well, it was bad enough to kill the Lord of life! Isaiah tells it straight: "He was pierced for our transgressions, he was crushed for our iniquities." And those two words "pierced" and "crushed" pretty well sum it up. So let there be no more talk about sins as mistakes in judgment or as little slipups or unfortunate choices. There was hell to pay that day at Calvary—hell to pay for mankind's sins. And that's the truth. It was our debt that was paid that day—paid with Christ's innocent suffering and death. It was our punishment that was upon him.

But that punishment was a healing punishment! "The punishment that brought us peace was upon him, and by his wounds we are healed." And, thanks to his unspeakable gift, God gives salvation to all who believe. Thanks to the completed sacrifice of the death of his Son, Jesus, there is peace and healing—and plenty of it—for this troubled world of ours. The cross then is not tragedy, but triumph, for there is peace and there is healing in the holy wounds of Christ for the likes of you and me. Each of us belongs to the yearning, longing mass of humanity for which our Savior gave his life. Each of us longs for peace, a peace that will silence the anxiety of our hearts and the turmoil of our minds.

The same God "who did not spare his own Son, but gave him up for us all—how will he not also, along with him, graciously give us all things?" (Romans 8:32). Forgiveness of sins, life, and salvation; strength in every tribulation; peace in all turmoil; hope for every despair—it's all yours! Bought at a place called Calvary, paid for in blood, promised to you at your baptism, distributed to you in Christ's Holy Supper—it's all yours! To each troubled heart and aching soul, he gives his peace, for "by his wounds we are healed."

> Sweet the moments, rich in blessing, which before the cross we spend, life and health and peace possessing from the sinner's dying friend. Lord, in loving contemplation fix our hearts and eyes on you till we taste your full salvation and your unveiled glory view. Amen.

Enemies of the Cross

For, as I have often told you before
and now say again even with tears,
many live as enemies of the cross of Christ.
Their destiny is destruction, their god is their stomach,
and their glory is in their shame.
Their mind is on earthly things.
(Philippians 3:18,19)

It's hard to think of anything more central to the Christian faith than the cross of Jesus Christ. That's why it's so shocking to come across the apostle Paul's observation in our text: "Many live as enemies of the cross of Christ." Yes, it's sad, but it's true. And it's just as true today as it was when St. Paul first penned these words by inspiration of the Spirit of God. Many of our fellowmen live as enemies of the cross of Christ. Their lives are a mess. Their values and morals are twisted, distorted—in fact, turned upside down. The apostle captures it in a nutshell: "Their glory is in their shame."

And right here we move from the pages of the Bible to the pages of our newspapers. Aren't those words, "their glory is in their shame," a precise description of exactly what is going on in the twisted and perverted world we live in today? As faith in God and his Word fades from the public arena, our world seems more and more bent on destruction. God has a word for all enemies of the cross, for all members of this culture, so set, as they are, on self-destruction: REPENT! Come back! Come back to the Father's house, where you belong, and to his welcoming embrace. Turn around before it's too late!

And God has a word for each of us—those who like to think of themselves as "the people of God." And that word too is REPENT! Our text, you see, is also a call to repentance for each of us. During this Lenten season, you and I have a special opportunity to look into the mirror of God's holy law and take an honest look at our lives and identify the idolatry that lurks deep within each of us, that is, in our sinful nature. Does your stomach, for example, tend to become your god—that is, do you tend to indulge yourself and fill whatever your sinful cravings require? Is your mind too often set on earthly things? Do you march to a different drummer than the world around you, or have you fallen into step with the ungodly? Are you willing to go against the grain and defy our sin-ridden culture, or have you become part and parcel of it? Are you so focused on the here and now that you don't think of the hereafter? Are you so hung up on the realities you can see and feel that you forget the unseen realities of the kingdom of God: his Holy Word and sacraments?

If so, it's time to repent. It's time for the truth. "If we claim to be without sin, we deceive ourselves and the truth is not in us. If we confess our sins, [God] is faithful and just and will forgive us our sins and purify us from all unrighteousness" (1 John 1:8,9). For our Lord Jesus turned his enemies into his friends by laying down his life for all people. By his cross he won our salvation, and in his death and resurrection, he has given us a whole new life to live. We have his word on it, and we stand firm in the Lord and the word of his grace.

> **Before you, God, the judge of all, with grief and shame I humbly fall. I see my sins against you, Lord, my sins of thought and deed and word. They press me sore; to you I flee: O God, be merciful to me! Amen.**

Loss Is Gain

*"If anyone would come after me, he must deny himself
and take up his cross and follow me."*
(Mark 8:34)

We Christians use crosses everywhere—in our churches, on our walls, on our stationery, in our lapels, around our necks. But is it possible that we have become immune to the cross? That the cross of Jesus has become old hat? That it has become just another decoration for us?

Jesus, in our text, has a lot to say about the cross. And we can rest assured that he's not talking about a symbol or a decoration. For Jesus lays it all on the line and gets up close and personal. He makes it clear that there is a cross in store for anyone who belongs to him by faith: "If anyone would come after me, he must deny himself and take up his cross and follow me." Yes, Jesus tells it straight. The problem is that we're not particularly keen on hearing what he has to say.

What Jesus had to say about the cross didn't sound very good to the disciples either. In fact, Peter took

Jesus aside and began to rebuke him. To Peter's way of thinking, it was a crazy plan that Jesus had outlined for himself: suffering, rejection, and death. Who in his right mind would set an agenda like that? And so Peter did what you and I would do. He took the Lord aside and tried to set him straight.

And haven't we all, at one time or another, attempted to do much the same thing—to set our Lord straight. "Lord, there must be some mistake. Why should I have cancer? Lord, why should I face this hardship? Why should it be my parent who is dying? Why should my spouse leave me? Why, Lord, why? There must be some mix-up here!" If you have ever felt something like that—and who among us hasn't?—the Lord Jesus has a word for you today. And it is a word about the cross.

"In this world you will have tribulation," Jesus warns us. The devil, the world, and our own sinful nature will see to it that our lives as children of God will be no picnic. Even God himself may lay a few obstacles in our paths too—just to help us to see him more clearly, to follow him more nearly, and to love him more dearly. "Take up your cross and follow me," Jesus says. Our own personal crosses, our particular hardships, pain, and losses are instruments of God's healing love. Through them God goes to work on us and leads us in the path of repentance and faith.

Jesus' loss was our gain. The loss of his life meant that everyone who trusts in him gains the forgiveness of sins, life, and salvation. Jesus Christ took all our sins with him into his death so that he might give us his life instead. He humbled himself and was obedient unto death—even the death of the cross. Secure in his forgiving love, we can see that loss is gain. For the only thing we have to lose is sin and death. And what we have to gain is his life and his peace in the forgiveness of our sins.

> **Graciously my faith renew. Help me bear my crosses, learning humbleness from you, peace mid pain and losses. May I give you love for love! Hear me, O my Savior, that I may in heaven above sing your praise forever. Amen.**

A Living Temple

But the temple he had spoken of was his body.
(John 2:21)

It was a remarkable claim when you stop to think about it: "Destroy this temple, and I will raise it again in three days." Just what was Jesus talking about anyway? Well, he wasn't talking about a construction project. No, the "temple" he was talking about was a living temple, his body. That's what John tells us. And then John goes on to inform us that after the resurrection the disciples made the connection: "After he was raised from the dead, his disciples *recalled* what he had said. Then they believed the Scripture and the words that Jesus *had spoken*." And that's our privilege as well: to believe the Scripture and the words that Jesus has spoken.

The temple for the Israelites was more than a beautiful place for worship. It was the very house of God. For God had put his name upon that place. There he received the prayers and praises of his people. And there he promised to meet them with his forgiveness and mercy. Yes, what a place that temple was!

Just think of it: a place where they could go to meet God personally.

Wouldn't it be wonderful to have a place you could go and connect with God? Wouldn't it be great to have God right there to hear your pain and to bear your burdens and to dry your tears and lift your spirits? Wouldn't it be wonderful to hear him speak to you? to give you his forgiveness? his healing? his life?

Israel's temple was, indeed, great, but it was only a copy of the real thing. For no building can contain God. And that's why a lot of people wonder just where God is to be found. Why doesn't he make himself known to us? Why doesn't he just show himself for once? After all, it gets lonely in this world of ours.

We want to meet God personally too. And we can. For we have a *living* temple, a place to connect with God. His name is Jesus Christ. In him God has taken up residence on earth. In him God himself has taken up our sorrows. In him God has opened up his heart to the whole world and removed forever the damning record of sin and the whole rotten load of sin's pain and misery. All this he nailed to Jesus' cross. And there on his cross, Jesus Christ was temple, priest, and sacrifice, all in one. And if you ever doubt the love of God or wonder if God could ever forgive you for what you've done, take a look at that sacrifice and doubt no more.

And if you ever wonder where God is in the midst of the confusion of life, then seek him where he has promised to be found. For Jesus Christ is alive and well and bends low to meet you in the oral proclamation of his good news, in the washing of water with his Word, and in the eating of his Holy Supper. We have a living temple—a place to meet God—and his name is Jesus Christ.

> **O my God, my Rock and Tower, grant that in your death I trust, knowing death has lost his power since you crushed him in the dust. Savior, let your agony ever help and comfort me. When I die be my protection, light and life and resurrection. Amen.**

Real Life

*"Whoever wants to save his life will lose it, but whoever
loses his life for me and for the gospel will save it."*
(Mark 8:35)

This is not double talk; this is the plain truth. This
is not a paradox; this is simple reality. Those who are
locked up in their own little worlds, with themselves as
their own gods, will, in the end, perish. That's what
Jesus is saying. On the other hand, those who lay that all
aside are the ones who will find real life and peace. And
real life is to be had, not for the taking, but for the
receiving. Real life is not something that you can grab
for yourself. You can only receive it as it is given—
freely, abundantly under the cross of Jesus.

For on that cross of his, he has purchased forgiveness and life. He has purchased real life, not the cheap
imitation stuff that passes for life in this world, but real
life that was purchased at the price of death—the death
of God himself, the sacrifice and stand-in for the sins of
the whole world. It was a violent, humiliating, dreadful
death that Jesus died on his cross. But that was the only

way that sin and death would loosen their damnable grip on the lives of all the world. And so that cross of his, so horrible and detestable in itself, has become for us a wonderful and beautiful thing. Yes, the very means of death has become the means of life for us all.

That's why we exult in the cross of Jesus and give it such prominent consideration during our Lenten meditation. For Jesus waged war on that cross of his! His cross was the sword he used to demolish sin and death for all eternity. It was the vehicle of salvation for the whole world.

Yet, there's one thing we seem to have trouble comprehending. Why Jesus had to die on his cross—that we can understand. But why we should have to take up a cross in our lives—that we have trouble seeing. We would prefer a life of comfort and ease. We'd like to believe that, with God on our side, life would be a bed of roses. But the fact is that sometimes God takes hardship and reversal, even pain and suffering, and uses it to do his gracious work in our lives—teaching us more of his love and grace as we follow him and take up our cross.

Now bearing our cross does nothing to remove our sin. Our suffering in any of life's deep, dark valleys simply can't remove our guilt. That was accomplished long ago at Calvary, once and for all. So we gladly shoulder the crosses of our lives out of love and thankfulness— because there we meet the One who took up his cross that we might live. We learn again and again that his grace is sufficient for us. We discover that his power is made perfect in weakness. And we find out that when we are weakest, that's when we are truly strong within the security of his love. In his Holy Supper, he gives us to eat of his very body broken and his very blood shed for our forgiveness. And he comes right into the middle of our fears and weaknesses as the Word is proclaimed in his holy name. He stands behind that Word of his, and in that Word is life, the very life of Christ.

> **Why should cross and trial grieve me? Christ is near with his cheer; never will he leave me. Who can rob me of the heaven that God's Son for me won when his life was given? Amen.**

The Word of God
The Passion of Our Lord Jesus Christ
Drawn from the Four Gospels
Second Sunday in Lent

Jesus in Gethsemane

Jesus and his disciples sang a hymn after they had eaten the Passover meal and the Lord's Supper. Then they left the upper room and headed for the Mount of Olives which was just outside the city of Jerusalem. It was already late at night.

On the way Jesus told his disciples, "This very night you will all be offended because of me. For the Scriptures say: 'I will kill the shepherd, and his sheep will be scattered.' But after I have been raised from the dead, I will go ahead of you into Galilee and meet you there."

Peter answered, "Even if all the others should fall away because of you, I will never fall away."

But Jesus replied, "Listen to what I tell you: This very night, before the rooster crows twice, you will deny me three times—saying that you don't even know me."

Even then Peter confidently replied, "Even if I have to die with you, I will never deny you." And all the other disciples said the same thing.

Jesus continued to walk along with his disciples. They crossed the brook Kidron and came to the Mount of Olives. On one of its slopes, there was an olive grove, a place called the Garden of Gethsemane. Jesus had often gone there in the past with his disciples when he wanted to be alone with them. Judas also had been there with Jesus many times before, so he knew the place well. As they reached the entrance, Jesus said to his disciples, "Sit down here while I go on ahead and pray. Pray that you will not fall into temptation."

Then he took Peter, James, and John along with him and went farther into the garden. Great grief and anguish came over him. He told his disciples, "My soul is so overwhelmed with sorrow that it's almost crushing me to death. Stay here and keep watch with me." Then he walked away from them, about as far as a man can throw a stone. He knelt down with his face to the ground and prayed that, if possible, the hour might pass from him. "Father, my Father," he prayed, "all things are possible for you. There is nothing you cannot do. Please take this terrible cup of suffering away from me. Yet not what I want, but what you want. Not my will, but yours be done."

Then he went back to the three disciples but found them sleeping, exhausted from grief and sorrow. So he said to Peter, "Why are you asleep? Couldn't the three of you stay awake and watch with me for one hour? You must stay awake and keep praying so that you won't fall into temptation. The spirit is willing, but the sinful flesh is weak."

Then Jesus went away and prayed a second time, saying, "O my Father, if it's not possible for me to get rid of this cup of suffering without drinking it, may your will be done."

When Jesus returned he found his disciples sleeping. They just couldn't keep their eyes open. And they didn't know what to say in answer to his questions. So he left them again and went away and prayed a third time, praying the same prayer as before. An angel came from heaven to strengthen him. And as his agony grew worse, he prayed all the harder. And his sweat looked like drops of blood falling to the ground.

When he came back to his disciples, he said to them, "Are you going to go on sleeping and resting all night? But look! The hour has come for the Son of Man to be betrayed into the hands of wicked men. Get up and get ready to go! Here comes the man who is going to betray me!"

Jesus is betrayed

Even while he was saying this, Judas arrived with a large crowd of men. Among them were Roman soldiers and men from the temple police force armed with swords and clubs. They also carried torches and lanterns so they could find their way in the night. They had been sent by the Jewish religious leaders—the chief priests, teachers of the law, and elders of the people—to arrest Jesus. Earlier Judas had worked out a signal with the soldiers and the police: "The man I kiss is the one you want. Grab him and hold him."

So as soon as he had a chance, Judas walked up to Jesus and said, "Greetings, Master!" and kissed him.

"Friend, why have you come?" Jesus asked him. "Judas, do you betray the Son of Man with a kiss?"

And since Jesus knew everything that was going to happen to him, he then turned to the crowd and asked, "Who are you looking for?"

"Jesus of Nazareth," they answered.

"I am Jesus of Nazareth," the Savior replied.

When Jesus said this, the men all backed away from him and fell to the ground. After they had struggled to their feet again, Jesus asked them once more, "Who are you looking for?"

And once more they said, "Jesus of Nazareth."

"I have told you," Jesus said, "that I am Jesus." Then pointing to his disciples, he added, "If you're looking for me, then let these men go their way." He said this so that what he had said earlier that night would come true: "I have not lost one of those you gave me."

Then the soldiers and temple police took him and made him their prisoner. When the disciples saw what was happening, they asked, "Lord, should we fight them with our swords?" Before Jesus could answer,

Peter pulled out his sword and swung at the high priest's servant, cutting off his right ear. The servant's name was Malchus.

"Stop it!" Jesus said. "Put your sword back in its case. For all those who take up the sword will perish by the sword. Shall I not drink the cup the Father has given me? Don't you know that I could ask my Father to send a whole army of angels to help and protect me, and he would send them at once? But then how would the Scriptures be fulfilled, which say that all that is happening now is part of God's plan?" And he touched the servant's ear and healed it.

Then Jesus turned to the chief priests and other leaders in the crowd and said, "Did you have to come out here with swords and clubs to capture me as if I was some terrorist or revolutionary? I was with you day after day teaching in the temple, and you never raised a hand against me then. But this is your hour—the hour when the power of darkness is in charge! All this has happened that the words of the prophets in the Scriptures might be fulfilled."

Then all the disciples deserted him and fled.

And there was one young man following Jesus who was only wearing a linen sheet wrapped around him. So when they tried to capture him, he slipped out of the sheet and ran away naked.

Then the soldiers and temple police tied Jesus' hands and led him away towards Jerusalem, where he would be put on trial for his life. They took him first to

Annas, who was still called "high priest," even though his son-in-law Caiaphas was now the real high priest. Caiaphas was the one who, at an earlier meeting of all the Jewish leaders, had told them that it was good that one man should die for the people.

The Sign of Conquest

For God was pleased to have all his fullness dwell in him,
and through him to reconcile to himself all things,
whether things on earth or things in heaven,
by making peace through his blood, shed on the cross.
(Colossians 1:19,20)

There is a note of sobriety and somberness about the Lenten season. And that is as it should be. The liturgical silences and the somber worship of Lent serve to underscore the profound tragedy of our sin and the awesome penalty that sin exacted: the very death of God! But the somberness of this season is tinged in victory. For the cross is actually not an emblem of defeat but the sign of conquest.

The cross, in and of itself, to be sure, wasn't much. In fact, it wasn't worth anything. And crucifixion victims were a dime a dozen to the Roman soldiers. Life was cheap to them and their commanding officers, and they could nail a man to a cross as easily as you or I squash a mosquito. So the cross itself wasn't all that extraordinary. And yet the cross of Jesus had tremendous power—but only because of the victim who hung there on it. Listen to what Scripture has to say about him who hung there: "For God was pleased to have all his fullness dwell in him."

Did you catch that? All the "fullness" of God dwelled in him. In other words, he is the One who made the stars and set the planets spinning in the first place—the One who called forth this infinite universe out of nothing at a single word. And yet, he allowed himself to hang there, naked and despised, the victim of the sins of man. Can you get your heart around the infinite love of this God of ours who would stoop so low for us all?

And now, because of Jesus, the cross is a most powerful sign, indeed. And if you've ever wondered what God is really up to in your life, then take a look at the cross. If you've ever wondered what God's will is for your life, then take a look at the cross. If you've ever wondered whether God is interested in you, or whether he really cares or actually loves you, then take a look at the cross. For through the cross of Jesus we come to know God and what he's truly like. For this is all we know of God and all we need to know: he is a God who dives right into the horror of our sin and death, taking it all upon himself and bearing it all away, even though it means his own death.

We don't like to talk about sin. We prefer to cover up sin or excuse it or pretend it isn't important. But the conquest of the cross means God kills sin by taking it with him into his death. The cross is no mere *emblem* of God's love, or the *possibility* for forgiveness, or the *potential* for meaning and hope for our lives. The cross is where Jesus tackled the real sin of our lives and purchased real forgiveness, "making peace through his blood, shed on the cross." And this peace, the Bible tells us, the world cannot give. A peace purchased with the blood of Jesus, backed up by his glorious resurrection, and presented now to you within his church.

Savior, when in dust to you low we bow in homage due, when, repentant, to the skies scarce we lift our weeping eyes. Oh, by all your pains and woe suffered once for us below, bending from your throne on high, hear our penitential cry! Amen.

The Light Has Come

> *"This is the verdict: Light has come into the world,*
> *but men loved darkness instead of light*
> *because their deeds were evil. Everyone who does evil*
> *hates the light, and will not come into the light*
> *for fear that his deeds will be exposed."*
> (John 3:19,20)

"I am the light of the world," says Jesus. But the world is too busy cursing the darkness to hear. We know what that's all about because we know that darkness too. With Saint Paul we can say, "I know that nothing good lives in me, that is, in my flesh." We know the struggle with our sinful nature. We know the stranglehold of temptation. We know the darkness that lurks deep within, that all too easily spills over in bitterness and hatred and anger, in the greed, lust, and envy of our sin.

And we also know the aftermath of sin: the loneliness and the guilt, the bitter pain and shame of it all—when all those promises we made to God to clean up our act and overcome our sin lie in shattered pieces all around us. And so we see why the world prefers darkness to light. The truth is, we do too. For in the darkness we cannot see the broken pieces of our shattered lives so clearly. And it seems so much safer to hide from God than to face him. As long as our deeds are hidden in darkness, we can pretend that things aren't all that bad, that we're decent people. And then we start to live a lie, trying to fool ourselves into believing that sin isn't all that bad.

Or maybe we fall prey to a more modern heresy: that once Jesus comes into your life, you should be able to get a grip on yourself and make something of your life. No wonder we sometimes begin to think that we have no sins to confess; that we can stand before God, secure on the basis of our own performance record. But the church is not a cozy club for spiritual know-it-alls and people who have it all together with God. Rather, the church is a hospital for sinners. It is the company of the walking wounded. Healing is to be found in the blood of Jesus Christ, God's Son, who has cleansed us from all sin. In his Christian church, he daily and richly forgives the sins of all believers. Our need to live a lie is over. There is no shame in confessing our sins. The only shameful thing is to pretend that we have no sins to confess.

Lent is a time of cleansing and renewal. We turn in repentance to God for forgiveness and healing in the righteousness and purity of the Lord Jesus Christ, finding redemption in his body and his most holy blood. "Light has come into the world," you see, and that light is Jesus Christ. On his cross he drank deeply of the darkness of death. But our darkness could not overcome his light. In his dying breath, he cried out in victory, "It is finished!" As it was then, so it is now in Jesus' name.

> **Glory be to Jesus, who in bitter pains poured for me the lifeblood from his sacred veins. Grace and life eternal in that blood I find. Blest be his compassion, infinitely kind. Lift we, then, our voices, swell the mighty flood; louder still and louder praise the precious blood! Amen.**

God's Blessings—and Curses

"Blessed are you when men hate you,
when they exclude you and insult you
and reject your name as evil, because of the Son of Man.
Rejoice in that day and leap for joy,
because great is your reward in heaven.
For that is how their fathers treated the prophets.
Woe to you when all men speak well of you,
for that is how their fathers treated the false prophets."
(Luke 6:22,23,26)

Something in this text doesn't sound right. We're used to hearing Jesus speak words of blessing. We're not accustomed to hearing him pronounce words of woe and punishment. We expect Jesus to give us promises of his care and protection. We're surprised when he threatens judgment.

In this text the Lord Jesus instructs his disciples on what it means to live as the baptized children of God in this world, what it means to be children of light in a world of darkness, what it means to belong to the kingdom of God while living in the kingdom of this world.

In other words, he is instructing them and us on how to find life in the midst of death.

The secret to such things lies in two key words: blessing and woe. Both come from God himself. Blessing comes from the gracious presence of God. Woe flows from his unswerving judgment against all evil. When Jesus speaks blessing, blessing happens. It's as simple and yet as wonderful as that. And when Jesus speaks woe, the curses and judgments of God are unleashed on all ungodliness and idolatry, on every evil, and on the evil one—who is the root of all evil.

"Woe to you who laugh now, for you will mourn and weep." As Jesus speaks, so it is. In the midst of our Lenten observance, his words are starkly sobering. For the truth is, we often laugh when we should weep. Our world has become a theme park, an entertainment culture in which people search constantly for something or someone to make them happy. So much so that we are in danger of "amusing ourselves to death," as one recent observer put it.

Make no mistake about it: we are in serious trouble. Wherever *feeling good* takes precedence over *being good*, we are in danger from the evil one. Wherever amusement and entertainment take the place of repentance and sorrow over sin, we have lost our first love. But those who weep now over sin and the results of sin will laugh; they find the joy of sins forgiven now and an eternity of joy in the world to come.

Already here in his kingdom, he gives us salvation, full and free, in the forgiveness of sins. And we have a share in the heavenly kingdom yet to come when we believe the Word he places into our ears and into our very mouths along with his true body and true blood. Through these means he gives his Holy Spirit, the down payment on the eternal joys yet to come. So for the sake of these things, we are prepared to endure suffering now, that we may know his perfect peace both now and to all eternity. For as Jesus speaks, so it is.

> **When over my sins I sorrow, Lord, I will look to you and hence my comfort borrow that you were slain for me. Your precious blood was offered for me, oh, most unworthy, to take away my guilt. Therefore I will forever give thanks continually, O Jesus, loving Savior, for what you did for me. Amen.**

Penitential Joy

Let us fix our eyes on Jesus, the author and perfecter
of our faith, who for the joy set before him
endured the cross, scorning its shame,
and sat down at the right hand of the throne of God.
(Hebrews 12:2)

"Let us fix our eyes on Jesus." Not a bad idea for Lent. There's just one thing: along with Jesus comes his cross. You can't have one without the other.

Most of us like to wear a cross now and then. It actually looks kind of nice on a lapel pin or a neck chain. But it's quite another story when it comes to taking the message of the cross to heart. For there is only one meaning to the cross: and that's death, pure and simple. It means, first of all, the death of God himself for the sins of the world. It also means the death of our sinful nature day by day. And let's face it, people aren't all that interested in death—not when death involves them anyway.

Yet Lent is not a downer, a depressing fascination with death and morbid things, some six-week sorrow bash in which we are led to feel sorry for Jesus. No! Lent is a time of repentance and renewal, a time of cleansing. Lent is a time of penitential joy. It was "for the joy set before him," after all, that Jesus endured the cross. It was for that joy that he endured the pain and scorned the shame and scoffed at the humiliation of it all.

Joy, you say? That's right. The sheer, unmitigated joy of lifting our burdens, bearing our sin, taking away our shame, and dying our death. His joy was simply that you and I might be cleansed and go free. And his cleansing is more than skin deep, for openly—before our brothers and sisters, before the unseen company of heaven, and most important before the great God Almighty himself—we say bluntly and plainly, "I confess that I have sinned in thought, word, and deed." We tell the truth before God. We lay before him our souls, our lives, and our all—not in order to pay him back for something he's done for us—but because these all belong to him. He has redeemed us with his body and purchased us with his most holy blood.

Redeemed and cleansed by that precious blood, my soul, my life, my all become clean and pure in the forgiveness of sins—living sacrifices, holy and acceptable to God through faith in Jesus Christ. All the vain things that charm us most, all the evil things we have ever done, all the hateful words we've ever spoken, all the wicked thoughts engraved deep within our sinful hearts, all the sins we can never purge from our memory—God has already blotted out forever in the blood of his precious Son.

It was for this joy that Jesus walked the road of his cross. Now you and I have the proof of his love in his preached Word. We taste his love in his holy meal, and there is joy once more. We are cleansed and set free in the total forgiveness of all our sins.

> Blest are they, forever blest, whose guilt is pardoned by their God, whose sins with sorrow are confessed and covered with their Savior's blood. How glorious is that righteousness that hides and cancels all their sins, while bright the evidence of grace through all their lives appears and shines. Amen.

Today You Shall Be with Me

*Then he [the criminal] said, "Jesus, remember me
when you come into your kingdom."
Jesus answered him, "I tell you the truth,
today you will be with me in paradise."*
(Luke 23:42,43)

It was an extraordinary scene. Two men condemned to die. Two men sharing a common fate: suspended on nails pounded through living flesh into a wooden cross. One of them punished justly—the other innocent of any and all charges lodged against him. But both of them under the condemnation of men and the curse of God. And near the end, the condemned criminal turns to the figure on the cross next to him—a naked, bleeding, empty husk of a man—and calls him king. "Jesus, remember me when you come into your kingdom."

We are that criminal today. We come, each of us, in different circumstances. Some content and filled to the brim with life and countless blessings. Some empty and hurting, fresh from the battlefields of life, with wounded hearts and empty souls. Others aching with the loss of someone we love. And still others wondering whether anything or anyone can ever bring comfort and peace to our distress. But whether we're happy or hurting, whether we're empty or full, all of us come to confront the final realities of sin and grace, time and eternity, death and life.

The prayer of that criminal is ours this day, for each of us, in his own way, needs deliverance: "Jesus, remember me." And Jesus surprises us just as he surprised the dying criminal at Calvary: "I tell you the truth, today you will be with me in paradise." "Today," Jesus replied. One might call that day at Calvary the inauguration of the kingdom of God, where Jesus began his reign. His throne was a cross, and his crown was made of thorns. There in his dying and rising again, he won the victory and snatched all of mankind out of the jaws of sin and death. It is true both here and now, and to all eternity. NOW is the time of God's favor; NOW is the day of salvation, for Jesus is present with his church.

Where the Word of Jesus is, there is Jesus. Where the Supper of the Lord is, there is Jesus. Where the Word and Supper of Jesus is, there heaven intersects with earth and eternity. And where the Word and Supper of Jesus is, there hearts are lifted up, sins are forgiven, and lives are restored. There slaves to sin and death are made servants of the heavenly King.

So NOW is the time. This very day and here and now, there is forgiveness and life and salvation in the name and for the sake of Jesus Christ. Here, by his

Word and authority, we are freed from bondage to sin and made new to live under him in his kingdom and to love and serve him in this world in perfect righteousness, innocence, and blessedness.

So let there be no mistake about it. This is your day. This is the day of God's favor and salvation for you, whoever you are. No matter what your sin, no matter how anxious your mind or how heavy your heart, no matter how deep your wounds, you are not alone. Christ's promise is for you, this day and always: "Today you shall be with me."

There is a fountain filled with blood— Immanuel was slain—and sinners who are washed therein lose every guilty stain. The dying thief rejoiced to see that fountain in his day. And there have I, as vile as he, washed all my sins away. Amen.

No Barrier to God

Those who passed by hurled insults at him,
shaking their heads and saying,
"So! You who are going to destroy the temple
and build it in three days,
come down from the cross and save yourself!"
(Mark 15:29,30)

What's the big deal about the cross and the tearing of a veil in the temple, anyway? Many couldn't care less. After all, what's so special about having access to God? You see, we have the idea that God's door is always open. And perhaps that's why there's a lot of shoulder shrugging about the cross. It just may be that people can't get it through their heads that there is a barrier between us and God, even though Isaiah stated it rather clearly long ago: "Your iniquities have separated you from your God; your sins have hidden his face from you, so that he will not hear" (Isaiah 59:2).

And yet we keep on thinking that sin isn't all that bad. God, however, reminds us that the situation is far worse than we might think. Sin is idolatry. It is open rebellion against him who created us. It is an attempt to live on our own without him. And to live without him, our Lord and God, is to die. Yes, our sin is a wall that does, indeed, separate us from God.

You and I know all about walls, for we spend a lot of time behind them, all of us. Some walls we ourselves have constructed—using bricks of anger and hatred and bitterness. Some walls have been built by others—perhaps out of strife and hatred, perhaps out of nothing more than busyness and the hectic pace of life. Whether we build the walls ourselves or someone else builds them, the loneliness and separation that results still hurts the same.

Such walls between people are, indeed, painful. But the ugliest, most hurtful wall of all is the wall between us and God. For there is no man so alone as the man who is alone with his sin. And that's the situation we have created for ourselves. Our sins have cut us off from God, and there is no way we can break through the barrier from our side.

But you and I have a God who breaks down barriers with a love so deep and strong that no barrier could stop it. He would not live in heaven without us. And he would not have us live on earth without him. So, bursting through the dividing wall, he came down here to take our guilt himself. He took all that guilt into his own body, bearing our sins, even though it killed him. And he won the victory by his death, so that there would be no more barriers, no more walls, no more pain and loneliness.

Now we can approach the awesome throne of God and speak to him like little children beloved by their father. Now we're alone no longer. For in his holy gospel and in his Holy Supper, this same Lord Jesus comes, and he comes to break down barriers and tear down walls. In his forgiving love, he invites the demolition of those barriers we have erected. And most wonderful of all—in the forgiveness of sins, he daily invites us to come into the very presence of his Father. In Jesus Christ the walls come tumbling down. Thanks be to God!

Through Jesus' blood and merit I am at peace with God. What, then, can daunt my spirit, however dark my road? My courage shall not fail me, for God is on my side. Though hell itself assail me, its rage I may deride. There's nothing that can sever me from the love of God, no want, no pain whatever, no famine, danger, sword. Though thousand foes surround me, for slaughter mark his sheep, they never shall confound me—the victory I shall keep! Amen.

The Word of God
The Passion of Our Lord Jesus Christ
Drawn from the Four Gospels
Third Sunday in Lent

The Trial before the High Priest

The soldiers and temple police who had arrested Jesus brought him to the high priest's house, where the Sanhedrin, the Jewish high council, was assembled. Now, when Jesus had been captured, all of the disciples had deserted him and run for their lives. Peter and John, however, recovered from their panic. And staying at a safe distance, they followed the crowd through the streets of Jerusalem to Caiaphas' house. They wanted to see what would happen to Jesus.

The two of them got to the high priest's house about the same time as Jesus was being led in. John was able to go into the courtyard right away because he was known to the high priest. But Peter had to wait outside at the gate. John then came back and spoke to the young servant girl on duty there, and she also let Peter in.

Meanwhile, Caiaphas had called together all the other members of the Sanhedrin to put Jesus on trial for his life. They had met several months earlier to talk about Jesus and his growing popularity among the people. And already at that time they had decided what they were going to do with him—sentence him to death.

So at this trial all they were trying to do was to find some evidence against Jesus that would justify giving the death penalty, but they couldn't find any. One after another came before the court and made false accusations against Jesus. But no two of them agreed, so their evidence couldn't be used. But finally, two men stepped forward and said, "We heard this man say, 'I am able to destroy the temple of God and rebuild it in three days. I will destroy this man-made temple and in three days will build another, not made by man.'" Yet even their testimony did not agree.

Then the high priest stood up and put this question to Jesus, "What about the charges these men are bringing against you? Aren't you going to answer them?" But Jesus kept quiet. He didn't say a single word.

Every attempt to prove Jesus guilty of wrongdoing had failed. Desperate to convict him, Caiaphas put another question to Jesus, this time under oath: "I charge you under oath by the living God: Tell us if you really are the Christ, the Son of God?"

Jesus answered, "I am. And I'm also telling you that one day you will see the Son of Man sitting at the right hand of God and coming on the clouds of heaven to judge the world."

The high priest tore his clothes and said, "Do we still need witnesses? You have heard his blasphemy yourselves! What's your verdict?" They answered, "He's guilty. He must die."

Then some of them began to spit on him and beat him with their fists. Others blindfolded him, slapped him in the face, and said, "You're a prophet who knows everything, aren't you? So tell us who hit you!" And the officers of the high court beat him and insulted him as they led him away.

In the meantime, Peter was outside in the court-yard, waiting to see how everything would turn out. He had joined a group of servants and temple police who were sitting around a charcoal fire they had built. The night was cold, and they were trying to keep warm.

The servant girl who had been on duty at the gate walked over and saw Peter warming himself. She looked at him closely in the light of the fire. Sure that she recognized him, she said, "You! You're one of those who was with Jesus of Nazareth. You're one of his disciples."

Peter, however, denied it. "I am not," he said. "I don't know what in the world you're talking about." Then Peter moved away from the fire and closer to the exit.

Another girl saw him there and said to those who were standing around, "This fellow is one of them. He was with Jesus of Nazareth." But again Peter denied it. This time he swore an oath and said, "I don't know the man."

A little later some other men approached Peter and said, "You've got to be one of his followers. You're a Galilean just as he is. Your accent gives you away." Then came a challenge from another direction. A relative of the man whose ear Peter had cut off in Gethsemane asked him, "Didn't I see you with Jesus in the garden? I'm certain you were there."

With that Peter began to curse and to swear. "I swear that I'm telling you the truth," he said. "Why, I don't even know this person you're talking about."

As soon as he said it, a rooster crowed a second time, and the Lord turned and looked straight at Peter. And then Peter remembered what Jesus had said to him: "Before the rooster crows twice, you will deny me three times." Torn with grief and remorse, Peter went out and wept bitterly.

As soon as it was morning, the Sanhedrin met officially to confirm the death penalty and to plan how they could get the Roman governor to confirm and carry out the sentence they had passed.

When Judas learned that the Sanhedrin had condemned Jesus to die, he felt sorry for what he had done. So he took the 30 silver coins back to the chief priests and the other members of the high council. "I sinned," he said, "when I handed over a man who hasn't done anything wrong at all and so put his life in jeopardy. Take your money back."

"What do we care about that!" they replied. "That's your problem." So Judas threw the 30 silver coins down on the floor of the temple. Then he went and hanged himself.

The chief priests picked up the coins and said, "This is blood money—money that's been used to get someone killed. So it's against the law to put it in the temple treasury." They talked the whole matter over and decided to use the money to buy the potter's field—the field where the potters dug their clay—and to make it into a cemetery to be used for the burial of poor strangers and foreigners who died while attending festivals in Jerusalem. And that is why to this day that field has been called the "Field of Blood."

In this way they fulfilled what was spoken by Jeremiah the prophet, saying, "They took the 30 silver coins, the price set on him by the people of Israel, and they used them to buy the potter's field."

The Tragedy and the Triumph

"O Jerusalem, Jerusalem,
you who kill the prophets and stone those sent to you,
how often I have longed to gather your children together,
as a hen gathers her chicks under her wings,
but you were not willing!
Look, your house is left to you desolate. I tell you,
you will not see me again until you say,
'Blessed is he who comes in the name of the Lord.'"
(Luke 13:34,35)

Triumph and tragedy: these are the two poles between which we sons and daughters of Adam and Eve have always lived on this side of eternity. What happened at the cross was nothing new. Jesus' treatment at the hands of the mob at Pilate's palace was just another instance of how Jerusalem had treated the prophets down through history. They were forever killing the prophets God sent them—just as they would deliberately send Jesus to his death. This is the *tragedy*, you see. He came to his own people, and his own people received him not.

But here is the *triumph*: that to all who did receive him, to them he gave power to become the children of God—born not of blood nor of the flesh nor of a husband's will, but born of God by Holy Baptism.

This theme of tragedy and triumph runs like a gold thread throughout the Scriptures. And it's absolutely vital that you get your mind and heart around both, or else you can never come to grips with the cross. Such things can be comprehended only as you and I are given them to see by the power of God's Holy Spirit, for they are spiritually discerned. Our natural mind, which is at enmity with God, can never, as a result, come to grips with the cross. And in and of ourselves, we cannot see the triumph that lies hidden behind the apparent tragedy.

The natural mind is forever looking for the thrill of victory and wants nothing to do with the agony of defeat. The natural mind keeps wanting to bypass the cross and go straight for the good stuff: glory, power, honor, and joy. Yet God would have us see that there is no glory apart from the cross. There is no power Christ has to give us that was not first shown in weakness. There is no honor he has achieved for us that was not won in dishonor. There is no joy he holds in store for us that was not first attained by sorrow. No human being could ever have dreamt up such a way of salvation. It's just not man's way. But it is God's way. And God's way is always the right way.

And so this holy season of Lent is tailor-made for the likes of us, so genuine and sincere in faith, and yet so hardened and complacent in our sin. It is a time for renewal and for cleansing. A time of repentance; a time for our vile hearts to turn from misbelief and despair and the great shame and vice of our sin to the righteousness and true holiness of the children of God, born again in the font of Christ to live before him in righteousness, innocence, and blessedness. It's a special time to come clean before our God and Father, openly confessing the truth and shame of our sin and receiving from him the full and free redemption purchased for us upon the cross of Christ. There is *no tragedy* in such confession, *only the triumph* of the entire forgiveness of our sins in Jesus' name.

> **I, a sinner, come to you with a penitent confession. Savior, show me mercy, too. Grant for all my sins remission. Let these words my soul relieve—Jesus sinners does receive. Amen.**

Foolishness

*For the message of the cross is foolishness
to those who are perishing,
but to us who are being saved it is the power of God.*
(1 Corinthians 1:18)

Lent is a time for each of us to consider what it means to follow One whose greatest achievement in life was his death. The conclusion many have already come to is that the cross of Christ is downright foolishness.

It just isn't logical that the all-powerful God would descend from his heavenly throne of glory to take on the lowly, feeble form of a human embryo, and then be born from his mother's body and be laid in a cattle trough. It just doesn't add up.

It just doesn't make sense that this perfect, sinless God-Man would take on the burden of living the perfect life for us by his baptism in the Jordan, absorbing the poison of our sin and death into that perfect, sinless body of his. No, it just doesn't add up.

It doesn't make sense—that the One who is the Lord of all life, the One who cannot die, the immortal

God should be laid low in death. It boggles the mind that the eternal Word from the Father, this cosmic king, should breathe his last and die in humiliation and shame and pain as he did. It just isn't rational that the Father would pour out his wrath on his beloved Son. It just doesn't add up. It makes no human sense. It's pure foolishness. And, humanly speaking, it does seem to be a dumb idea that you should live by dying.

And yet that's the way it is, isn't it? "To us who are being saved" the message of the cross "is the power of God." We don't have to apologize for the cross. We don't need to try and make it more acceptable to human logic. In fact, it can't be done. It's simply impossible to prop up the cross with enough human logic so that it makes sense. There's really no defending the cross; it can't be defended. It can only be proclaimed. And that's what the apostle does. "We preach Christ crucified," he writes.

There is no other message to preach, you see. For there is no other way out from under the human predicament, no other way we could escape the eternal hellfire we deserve than for God to act in the dramatic and decisive way he did. Stepping here into this world of ours, he took matters into his own hands. Shouldering our burdens and carrying our sorrows, he bore our sins—taking them in his own body to his cross. Christ died our death on that cross of his. And since Jesus Christ is God, God died. Nothing else would do. There was no other way.

That's the long and the short of the cross. And so there is no better way for you and for me to live than to live under the cross of him who died so that we could live. His cross is anything but foolish. For us it is the very power of God for salvation. Thanks be to God!

Drawn to the cross, which you have blessed with healing gifts for souls distressed, to find in you my life, my rest, Christ crucified, I come. Amen.

Repentance and Faith, Forgiveness and Life

For as in Adam all die,
so in Christ all will be made alive.
(1 Corinthians 15:22)

That which is born of the flesh is flesh, God tells us. That is, the sin within the parent is passed on to the child. For the sinful mind is enmity against God. So it is now, and so it will always be, for so it was in the beginning. "In *Adam* all die." That's the unmitigated truth. Born into this world of sinful parents, we are all sinful people from the time of our conception. That's the sad reality.

But there's more. God also tells us that "as in Adam all die, so in Christ all will be made alive." We have been *born again* into a living hope. People have always had a hard time understanding what that means—being *born again*. Some ignore it, considering it only a figure of speech. Others insist *being born again* is some kind of spiritual experience by which people willfully choose to accept Jesus by their own power.

Jesus, however, explained that this rebirth, this *being born again*, is a birth "by water and the Spirit." In other words, it is the rebirth of Holy Baptism. And so it's not a matter of choice any more than our physical birth was. For by water and the Spirit, our gracious God begets us new as his sons and daughters and brings us into his own family, giving us all the rights and privileges of his inheritance: the forgiveness of sins, rescue from death and the devil, and eternal life to all who believe.

And that is precisely what we need. What else can keep us on the straight and narrow when everyone else seems to be wobbling all over? Repentance and faith; forgiveness and life. As baptized children of our heavenly Father, we return to Baptism each day by repentance and faith, receiving forgiveness and life.

Repentance, that's the ticket for Lenten meditation. Perhaps one of the reasons you and I just limp along in the Christian life is that we've developed an immunity to repentance. Only rarely are we moved deep down inside by the hopelessness of our sin and our helplessness before the judgment seat of God. We have hardened our hearts against the Word of God; we have time and again refused to repent and have continued merrily along in our sin.

In repentance and renewal, we return to Baptism. We turn with sorrow from our sin-sodden lives and find a whole new life in Christ Jesus our Lord. He didn't go to the cross for nothing, you know. It was *for you* that he was made to be sin. It was *for you* he suffered the agonies of the cross. It was *for you* he bled and breathed his last, and *for you* he died. That you might be made new in him. Not once, but repeatedly, over and over again as all your sins are first put to death with him by contrition and repentance; and then as he wipes out your sin, by the word of his forgiveness, making you new and whole, setting you free to live a life that is new and fresh and clean and holy—with a holiness not your own, but from God himself.

> **But Christ, the second Adam, came to bear our sin and woe and shame, to be our life, our light, our way, our only hope, our only stay. We thank you, Christ; new life is ours, new light, new hope, new strength, new powers. This grace our every way attend until we reach our journey's end. Amen.**

The Mind of Christ

Let this mind be in you, which was also in Christ Jesus.
(Philippians 2:5 KJV)

What would Jesus do? Perhaps you've seen that question or the acronym WWJD engraved on bracelets or printed on T-shirts. It's a popular question, one that's become the byword of many a Christian teenager.

What would Jesus do? It's a good question. And it's true: if more people would just ask that question before they acted, this world would be a better place to live. There's just one problem with the question. One could take it to imply that Jesus is distant and removed; that you and I have to figure out for ourselves what Jesus would do in our situation and then proceed to do it on our own. The question sounds very godly, but after all is said and done, it's just a motto. The apostle Paul gives us something better than a motto, he gives us a reality: "Let this mind be in you, which was also in Christ Jesus."

"What would Jesus do?" is not as important a question as "What *did* Jesus do?" During this Lenten season, we see clearly that Jesus was made to be our sin that we might be made the righteousness of God in him. All the bitter events of the cross were part of God's deliberate plan to make rebels into children, to make sinners into saints, to give us a whole new life to live! That new life is the life we live in Jesus. More precisely, it is the life that Jesus lives in us. For being baptized into Christ, you and I have put on Christ. Daily, by repentance, the old Adam in us is drowned and dies, and a new man emerges to live before God in righteousness and true holiness. And that new man looks surprisingly like Jesus.

So the question is really this: "What *is* Jesus doing?" Where is he now at work in my life in the power and presence of his Holy Spirit to root out sin in me and deal it to death, that he himself might be my light and life? We have the mind of Christ, you see—for Jesus Christ himself is alive and well in the midst of his church. By his living Word and in his Holy Sacrament, he dwells, not merely in high heaven, exalted at the Father's right hand, but also down here among us. *What is Jesus doing for you and in you?* **That** is the question. That's the mind of Christ, you see.

When I am tired of giving and giving and getting nothing in return; when it seems that others are taking advantage of my kindness, and I am getting nowhere; when it seems time to assert myself and tell everybody else where to get off, what should I do? What is the mind of Christ? We can see Jesus, his hands wet from the basin, his body wrapped in a towel, looking up from bended knee, saying: "If I then, your Lord and Teacher, have washed your feet, you also ought to wash one another's feet." Such is the mind of Christ, you see.

As you draw on the nourishment of his living Word and eat and drink his life-giving body and blood, the life of Jesus Christ himself throbs within you. Let this mind be in you, which is in Christ Jesus. "What is Jesus doing?"—that's the question. We live no longer for ourselves but for him who died for us and now lives forever!

> **Jesus, your boundless love to me no thought can reach, no tongue declare. Dwell in my heart eternally, and reign without a rival there. To you alone, dear Lord, I live. Myself to you, dear Lord, I give. Amen.**

The Plot Thickens

At that time some Pharisees came to Jesus
and said to him, "Leave this place
and go somewhere else. Herod wants to kill you."
He replied, "Go tell that fox, 'I will drive out demons
and heal people today and tomorrow,
and on the third day I will reach my goal.'"
(Luke 13:31,32)

There's something very comfortable about Lent: somehow it's so predictable and so familiar, like watching a classic biblical film on late-night TV. We've seen it all before. We know the plot, and we know the conclusion. We know that every year during the church's Lenten journey, we'll watch with Jesus while he is attacked by his enemies, arrested under false pretenses, convicted under trumped-up charges, and hung up to die. And finally we know that three days later he will burst out of his tomb into life again. Yes, we know the story line well.

Yes, we've heard it all before. But we need to meditate on it yet again. We need to take yet another look.

For there is a divine drama unfolding in the passion narrative—and each of us has a starring role. And the story is not over. The action continues still today. The drama unfolds every Lord's day as our Savior dispenses the forgiveness, life, and salvation he earned for us so long ago and so far away.

And it's a real-life story, this drama, filled with just the sort of twists and turns that make up life in the real world. "Herod wants to kill you," they told Jesus. That's pretty direct. It hits you right between the eyes. It has the sharp, blunt sting of reality to it. And many of us know how this sudden, stinging cruelty of life can come crashing in just like that—like when the doctor says, "I'm sorry to tell you, but it's cancer." Or when the boss calls you in and says, "We're cutting back around here, and we're going to have to let you go." Or it could be a hundred other things. The script varies a great deal, but the story always seem to unfold the same way in the drama of life. There comes a time in everyone's life when the plot thickens.

So also the plot thickened for Jesus. Yet, he was not a helpless pawn in the hands of Herod. And that's the point, of course. "No man takes my life from me," Jesus said. "I lay it down of my own accord." And that's exactly what he did. He was crucified for us in the last act of God's divine drama. At that painful, lonely and humiliating cross, Jesus Christ laid down his life for us. His death meant our life.

So when the plot thickens in your life, there is healing in the blood of Christ in his holy church. So come.

Through the preaching of his gospel and the administration of his Holy Sacrament, Jesus Christ continues to lift sorrowing spirits, heal broken hearts, unburden guilty consciences—making us new and whole again within the shelter of his love. Come, be healed, and live!

When life's troubles rise to meet me, though their weight may be great, they will not defeat me. God, my loving Savior, sees them. He who knows all my woes knows how best to end them. Amen.

A Penetrating Word

The word of God is living and active.
Sharper than any double-edged sword,
it penetrates even to dividing soul and spirit,
joints and marrow;
it judges the thoughts and attitudes of the heart.
Nothing in all creation is hidden from God's sight.
Everything is uncovered and laid bare before the eyes
of him to whom we must give account.
(Hebrews 4:12,13)

It's not a particularly comfortable feeling to be told in no uncertain terms that you're a sinner. But it's the truth. And it's for our own good. God, you see, does exactly that. He makes us uncomfortable. In fact, he drives us to despair. But he does so in order to bring us his comfort and consolation. For whenever he wants to lift us up, he first puts us down. And whomever he wants to make alive, he first kills. And that he might raise up the new man by his gospel, he first slays our old sinful nature with his law. That's the way it works with the Word of God.

Before God can restore us, he must first bring us to our knees in repentance. It's no fun, that experience. It's not pleasant being sliced open and having our thoughts revealed and our hearts exposed. But nothing else will do. The sacrifices of God are a broken spirit. A broken and contrite heart he will not despise. And so it is that when we look into our hearts with the clear light of the law of God, the little masquerade we've been playing before God is then shown up for what it is. Every vile thought, every hateful word, all the bitterness and resentment of our selfish souls, all the hurt and the pain we've caused others, the innumerable ways we've grieved our just and holy God—the whole dreadful lot of it is shown up for what it clearly is: damnable sin.

Yet during this Lenten season, our God has another word for us. He is the Word made flesh; Jesus Christ, the Son of God. And there on his cross and in his suffering, death, and burial, he was bearing all our sins in his own body and taking them all away with him into that death and grave of his. This Jesus, the Son of God, is a human being with flesh like ours—in fact, like us, he has been tempted in every way just as we are, yet without sinning. And he has gone ahead of us to the Father's throne.

Now we too may come before that heavenly throne. We may come into his presence, not with fear and trembling because of our sin, but boldly, with confidence—clothed not in our own righteousness, but in the righteousness purchased for us by Jesus' cross and death. We come before his throne of grace boldly, with confidence, to receive mercy and find grace to help us in our time of need. And whatever your need may be—whether it's a need of body or heart or soul—we may all rest assured our Father in heaven knows what it is.

So quit your fretting and fussing. Quit the mad, hectic pace of your everyday life, and find here something new and extraordinary and transcendent. Find calm in your chaos, peace in your tumult. Take your rest this day in the very presence of God. For Jesus Christ is your rest. He is present in his Holy Word and Sacrament. And you will find rest and refreshment for your souls in him.

What God ordains is always good. His will is just and holy. As he directs my life for me, I follow meek and lowly. My God indeed in every need knows well how he will shield me. To him, then, I will yield me. Amen.

The Word of God
The Passion of Our Lord Jesus Christ
Drawn from the Four Gospels
Fourth Sunday in Lent

Jesus before Pilate

When the Jewish leaders had bound Jesus, they led him from Caiaphas to the palace of Pontius Pilate, the Roman governor—the only person who had the power to put someone to death. But they refused to go into Pilate's palace. He was a Gentile, and they wanted to keep themselves ceremonially clean so that they could join in eating the Passover meal that afternoon.

So Pilate came out to them and asked, "What charge do you bring against this man?"

"If he weren't a criminal," they answered, "we wouldn't have brought him here for you to judge."

"Take him then and judge him by your law," Pilate shouted.

"But," the Jews objected, "your government doesn't allow us to put anyone to death." They said this so that what Jesus had told his followers earlier about the way he was going to die would come true.

Pilate then asked them what Jesus had done to deserve the death penalty. Knowing that they could not tell Pilate that Jesus was guilty of a religious matter like blasphemy, the Jewish leaders started to accuse Jesus of things that were crimes against Roman law. They said, "We have evidence that proves that this man has been stirring up trouble among our people. He has been telling them not to pay their taxes to your government. And besides that, he claims that he is their Messiah, their king."

Pilate went back inside the palace and had his men bring Jesus to him. "Are you the king of the Jews?" he asked.

"Is that your idea," Jesus asked, "or did others talk to you about me?"

"I'm certainly not a Jew, am I?" Pilate replied. "Your own people and the chief priests turned you over to me. What have you done?"

Jesus said, "My kingdom is not like the kingdoms of this world. If it were, then my subjects would have fought to keep me out of the hands of my Jewish enemies. But my kingdom is not of this world."

"You are a king, then?" Pilate asked quickly.

Jesus answered, "You are right in saying that I am a king. I was born and came into the world for one reason, one purpose—to bring the truth to the world. Everyone that is of the truth hears my voice."

"What is truth?" Pilate sneered. Without waiting for an answer, he went back out to the Jews and said to them. "I find no fault in this man. He has done nothing to deserve death."

But the chief priests and elders were not ready to give up. They just kept on pressing their charges more vehemently, talking louder and louder, and raising one accusation after another against Jesus: "He's stirring up the people all over Judea to turn against your government. That's what he's been teaching them. He started out in Galilee, and now he's come all the way down here to Jerusalem."

On hearing this, Pilate asked if Jesus was a Galilean. When he learned that Jesus belonged under Herod's jurisdiction, he sent him to Herod so he could decide the case. Fortunately, Herod was in Jerusalem at the time.

Herod was very glad to see Jesus. He had heard a lot about him, and he hoped that this would give him a chance to see Jesus perform a miracle. Herod asked Jesus one question after the other, but Jesus didn't answer. Nor did he do any miracles. All the while the chief priests and other Jewish leaders were standing there, vehemently accusing Jesus. Herod then allowed his soldiers to mock and ridicule Jesus. They dressed him in a gorgeous robe, such as kings wear, and pretended to honor him as a king. Then Herod sent Jesus back to Pilate. On that day Herod and Pilate became friends. Before that they had been enemies.

Jesus is sentenced to death by Pilate

Pilate then called the Jewish leaders and the people together once again and told them, "You brought this man to me. You accused him of trying to get the people to turn against my government. But I have examined him right here before your eyes. And I don't find him guilty of a single one of the crimes you accuse him of. Nor did Herod, because he sent him back to us. So it's perfectly clear that he has done nothing for which he should be sentenced to death. So, I will have him punished and then release him."

Now at the Passover festival, it was the governor's custom to set free one prisoner—one the people chose. It was a way of winning favor with the Jews. And this particular year he had a notorious prisoner named Barabbas. Barabbas was behind bars for starting a riot, as well as for murder. And Pilate knew full well that Jesus was innocent, and that the chief priests had handed Jesus over to him because they were jealous of him. So he said to the crowd, "It's customary for me to release one prisoner during the Passover. Now which one do you want me to set free for you? Barabbas or Jesus, who is called Christ?"

The chief priests and elders persuaded the crowd to ask for Barabbas and to kill Jesus.

Pilate asked them again, "Which of the two do you want me to release to you?"

The people screamed out as with one voice, "Away with this man, and release Barabbas for us."

While Pilate was sitting in the judgment seat, he received this message from his wife: "That man is innocent. He hasn't done anything wrong. Don't have anything to do with him. I have suffered much over him today in a dream."

Then Pilate turned to the crowd once again and said, "Then what shall I do with Jesus who is called Christ?"

"Crucify him!" they all shouted. "Crucify him! Crucify him!"

But Pilate still wanted to set Jesus free. So he took Jesus and had him whipped until his back was torn and bloody. He had the entire regiment of his soldiers gather around Jesus to mock him. The soldiers took off his clothes and made him wear a purple robe. Then they twisted some thorn branches together into the shape of a crown and jammed it down on his head and put a stick for a scepter in his right hand. Then one by one they got down on their knees in front of Jesus and said, "Hail, king of the Jews!"

Pilate went outside again and said to the Jews, "Now I am going to bring Jesus out to you so that you will know that I don't find him guilty of any crime at all." So Jesus came out, still wearing the crown of thorns and the purple robe. And Pilate said to the crowd, "Behold the man!"

But when the chief priests and their officials saw Jesus, they began to chant, "Crucify him! Crucify him!"

Pilate told them, "You take him and crucify him because I don't find him guilty."

The Jews answered, "We have a law, and according to our law he ought to die, because he claimed to be the Son of God."

When Pilate heard this, he was even more afraid. Once again he took Jesus back into the palace. "Where do you come from?" he asked, but Jesus didn't answer. This angered Pilate, and he growled, "Do you refuse to talk to me? Don't you know that I have the power to crucify you or the power to release you?"

Jesus answered, "You wouldn't have any power at all over me if God hadn't given it to you. Therefore the one who handed me over to you is guilty of a greater sin."

Overwhelmed at Jesus' answers Pilate kept on trying to find some way to set Jesus free. But the Jews kept shouting, "If you set this man free, you are no friend of Caesar's. Anyone who claims to be a king has set himself against Caesar."

When Pilate heard this, he brought Jesus out and sat down in the judge's seat in a place that is called the Stone Pavement, or, in Aramaic, *Gabbatha*. It was about the sixth hour. He said to the Jews, "Behold your king."

But they shouted fiercely, "Take him away! Take him away! Crucify him!"

"Shall I crucify your king?" Pilate asked.

"We have no king but Caesar," the chief priests answered.

Pilate saw that he was getting nowhere, and he realized the whole situation might set off a riot. So he took water and washed his hands for everyone to see. "I will not take the blame for killing this good man," he said. "This man's death is your responsibility!"

Then all the people responded, "Let his blood be on us and on our children!"

Then Pilate, bowing to the pressure and wishing to satisfy the crowd, gave in to their demands. He released Barabbas and had Jesus flogged. He then surrendered Jesus to their will to be crucified. The soldiers of the governor took off the purple robe and put his own clothes back on him. Then they led him out to crucify him.

Repentance and Cleansing

If we say that we have no sin,
we deceive ourselves, and the truth is not in us.
If we confess our sins,
he is faithful and just to forgive us our sins,
and to cleanse us from all unrighteousness.
(1 John 1:8,9 KJV)

During this holy season of Lent, we come face-to-face with things lasting and eternal—the truly lasting things of the kingdom of God and the fellowship of the holy Christian church, the communion of saints. That's why our gracious God is always calling us out of ourselves to live in union with him and in communion with his church. He loves us too much to let us remain wrapped up in self. That's why he went searching through Eden, calling out, "Adam, where are you?" That's why he sent prophet after prophet to his beloved people Israel, to call them repeatedly to repentance. That's why he "so loved the world, that he gave his only begotten Son, that whosoever believeth in him should not perish, but have everlasting life" (John 3:16 KJV).

Yet, in every age there has been a tendency for Christians to grow lazy and complacent, to settle in and grow comfortable with things that ought to make them extremely uncomfortable: the mad pursuit of pleasure, the endless pursuit of more things, and conversely, the failure to seek after godliness and contentment. We've come to accept such things as normal. We've begun to view greed and envy as perfectly ordinary. And we're getting to the point where our standards of right and wrong are about as pliable as putty. With immorality and perversion becoming standard public entertainment fare, we care less and less about how we live our lives. And the gospel, for far too many Christians, has become trite and empty, just a nice, but sappy, sentiment such as you might find on a greeting card.

You and I must examine our hearts and lives to see if that is so among us. Has the gospel become just another pious sentiment, making very little difference in how we live each day? How this could be among those who bear the name of Christ is a disgrace, of course. But if it's true, we must admit it. If we say we have no sin, we lie. The sooner we face the truth, the better off we'll be. But if we confess our sins, God is faithful and just to forgive our sins and cleanse us from all unrighteousness.

And it's time, high time, to confess our sins. For the demands of the law have been met in the cross. The ultimate death penalty has been leveled against all mankind and has been carried out on the ultimate sacrifice: God himself. Now there is no more need to go on wallowing in past guilt or present struggle. Now there is no need to go on licking our wounds and trying to patch ourselves together as best we can. For in Jesus Christ there is mercy. And he extends his mercy to us. That's the good news. The same Lord Jesus who was wounded for us pours out his healing love in the forgiveness of sins announced in his holy gospel, eaten in his Holy Supper. And that mercy is yours in Jesus Christ.

> **My Savior, wash me clean with your most precious blood, that takes away all sin and seals my peace with God. My soul will rest securely, for you still love me dearly. Now I find full salvation and freedom from damnation. Without you, lost, defiled by sin, my Savior, wash me clean. Amen.**

Bad Things and Good People

Now there were some present at that time who told Jesus
about the Galileans whose blood
Pilate had mixed with their sacrifices.
Jesus answered, "Do you think that these Galileans
were worse sinners than all the other Galileans
because they suffered this way? I tell you, no!
But unless you repent, you too will all perish."
(Luke 13:1-3)

If there is any question in life that turns us all into philosophers, it's the age-old one involving the problem of evil: "If God is good, why is there evil? Or, to put it another way, what can a good and gracious God intend by allowing calamities to fall upon his children?" Why the "bad guys" get theirs is something we can all understand. But when tragedy strikes the "good guys," we get a bit uptight. "Why can't God be fair?" we wonder. "Where is the justice in this?"

Listen to what Jesus says about bad things and good people: "Do you think that these Galileans were worse sinners than all the other Galileans because they suffered this way? I tell you, no! But unless you repent, you too will all perish." We keep thinking that we ought to be rewarded for good behavior and punished for bad behavior. But that's not the way it works in the kingdom of God.

If you want to see how God operates, just take a look at the cross where God meted out the just penalty for sin. *God punished the wrong guy!* Jesus Christ, God's Son, was without sin. He had done nothing wrong. But at the cross God balanced the scale of justice. All the weight of all the sins of all the people in all the world who have ever lived or ever will live was placed on him. And the weight of that guilt killed him. Bad things happened to a good man. And in the death and resurrection of Jesus Christ, the good things of God were passed on to all the bad people of the world who repent and believe in him: things like forgiveness of sins, life, and salvation.

Jesus tells us plainly, "Unless you repent, you too will all perish." That's the message of Lent, and it's a message for every one of us. For each of us, in his own way, stands guilty before God. Despite our good reputations and the admiration of our peers, each of us is as guilty as sin. We stand condemned by the evil things we have done and by the good things we have left undone.

This holy season of Lent is as good a time as any to repent—to lay aside the false bravado and the empty pride and the slick veneer that talks like a smug Pharisee: "God, I thank you that I am not like others." And then simply to stand before our God and confess the naked truth: "I, a poor miserable sinner, confess to you all my sins and iniquities with which I have ever offended you and justly deserved your punishment now and forever."

Unless we repent, we will all perish. But thank God it is also true that he commends his love towards us in that while we were yet sinners, Christ died for us. And there is now no condemnation for those who are in Christ Jesus. Thanks be to God!

Chief of sinners though I be, Christ is all in all to me. All my wants to him are known. All my sorrows are his own. Safe with him in earthly strife, I await the heavenly life. Amen.

Take Heart

"You will leave me all alone. Yet I am not alone,
for my Father is with me. I have told you these things,
so that in me you may have peace.
In this world you will have trouble.
But take heart! I have overcome the world."
(John 16:32,33)

Jesus tells his disciples that even if they all would leave him, the Father would still be with him. And yet, when Jesus got to the cross, he died alone—abandoned even by the Father. It had to be that way. If Jesus is truly the sin-bearer for all the world; and if even one sin is enough to remove us forever from the presence of God; then it should not shock us that Jesus was literally God-forsaken, abandoned by God, left out there to die on his cross all alone. You can't really understand the despair of the cross until the cry of Jesus sinks down deep into your bones: "My God, my God, why have you abandoned me?"

Some of us have experienced the loneliness of a cross we have to bear. Some won't go along with the crowd in their lifestyle and so find themselves on the outside looking in. Others refuse to cut corners on ethical issues, to wink at improprieties at work, or to look the other way while some people play fast and loose with company policy. Others know loneliness in a more personal way. There is a famine in our busy world: a friendship famine. We've become so isolated and involved in our own little worlds that we have precious few people who understand the deepest yearnings of our hearts. And there comes a time when we need someone to understand and to care, and then we find that we're left high and dry. Now perhaps we've never labeled that "loneliness," but that's what it is.

Yet these kinds of loneliness are nothing when compared to the loneliness of guilt. The Lutheran martyr Dietrich Bonhoeffer wrote: "He who is alone with his sin is utterly alone." The devil is a master at convincing us of this. He takes perverse pleasure in feeding our guilt. "You're a damned sinner," he reminds us time and time again. "You call yourself a Christian? Christians don't think the way you think and don't act the way you act!" he accuses. "How could God ever love you after what you've gone and done?" is the devilish question aimed at our wavering hearts. Yes, the loneliness of guilt is the most sinister loneliness of all, for guilt drives a wedge between us and God and leaves us all alone with our sin.

But there is no need for us to be alone with our sin anymore. We can confess our sin to the Savior; he knows the shame of it already. He took all the misery and pain, shame and death of it with him into his death on his cross. "Take heart," he says to you—no matter who you are, no matter what you have done, no matter how lonely the road you are walking. For you are not alone. In his Word and Sacrament, Christ comes to you—Christ, who knows what loneliness really is. And he means exactly what he *says:* "Take heart! I have overcome the world."

> **I trust in him with all my heart; now all my sorrow ceases. His words abiding peace impart; his blood from guilt releases. Free grace through him I now obtain; he washes me from every stain, and pure I stand before him. Amen.**

Signed, Sealed, and Delivered

Here is a trustworthy saying:
If we died with him, we will also live with him;
if we endure, we will also reign with him.
If we disown him, he will also disown us;
if we are faithless, he will remain faithful,
for he cannot disown himself.
(2 Timothy 2:11-13)

The death of Jesus is not just an *illustration* of God's grace. The cross was no mere *object lesson* of God's love for us. Rather, the death of Jesus on his cross is *concrete proof* that God stepped in, in person, to fill the shoes of the sinner—submitting himself to death itself, the humiliating death of the cross. Even as Jesus breathes his last, the bodies of the dead revived and the tombs of the dead opened up. The day Jesus died, you see, was actually a rehearsal for the Last Day, judgment day. And his death was actually the beginning of the end for death, hell, and the grave. Out text is a glorious reminder that death, since it means the death of sin, actually brings life. And you can count on it.

There's not too much in this world you can really count on when you get right down to it. Job security, personal property, investments—all of them can go up in smoke, just like that. Even the most sincere of human promises are often broken. The precious flames of human love and concern that warm our hearts may flicker out and die. But there is one promise that doesn't waver. "This is a trustworthy saying," the apostle writes: "If we died with him, we will also live with him." This is the promise of One who endured hours of bitter agony on his cross to be able to tell you this. He was abandoned by his Father, so you can be held safe and secure in the Father's arms forever. This is *his* promise, a promise literally written in blood—the very blood of God: "If we died with him, we will also live with him."

"But what about our sin?" we say. What about our faithlessness, the times we denied our Lord by our disinterest or callousness, the times we've treated him and his Word with casual disregard or even outright contempt? What about the times we've denied him by turning our backs on him or by failing to stand up and be counted? Might he now deny us? That won't happen. The Lord will never abandon us to the death we deserve. Jesus Christ is the Lord of life, you see. He can't deny himself. He is the way and the truth and the LIFE. His cross, though the means of death for him, is the means of life for us. There is no sin gross enough, no guilt horrendous enough, no shame deep enough to get between us and God.

Our Lord Jesus has written the final chapter on the whole sordid story of our sin. This is the blessed reality signed, sealed, and delivered to every believer in Christ. Signed at his cross, sealed in Baptism, and delivered in the word of the gospel absolution. He remains forever faithful, even when we are faithless. He remains our Savior and our Lord. Of that we can be sure.

Baptized into your name most holy, O Father, Son, and Holy Ghost, I claim a place, though weak and lowly, among your saints, your chosen host, buried with Christ and dead to sin. Your Spirit now shall live within. Amen.

Bearing the Cross

Then Jesus said to his disciples,
"If anyone would come after me, he must deny himself
and take up his cross and follow me.
For whoever wants to save his life will lose it,
but whoever loses his life for me will find it."
(Matthew 16:24,25)

Did you hear that? Did you get it? Jesus invites us to discipleship by saying that following him is going to involve self-denial and bearing the cross. Well, one thing's for sure. You can't accuse Jesus of mincing words. He lays it right out there for all of us to see and hear, "If anyone would come after me, he must deny himself and take up his cross and follow me."

It's not too hard to take up your cross "in theory." But it's quite another when it's the real thing. The cross Jesus faced was a real cross, a cross on which he shouldered all the misery of mankind, a cross on which he bore the whole stinking mess of our guilt. And the death he died on that cross was a real death. It meant the end, once and for all, of the power of sin to condemn. But that didn't make dying that death any easier. Jesus died a real death, our death, in fact. And it was the death of the cross. That is the cross he invites us to bear, a real cross.

Now, we can make our own choices and try to have things *our* way, or we can take up our crosses and have things *his* way. But we can't have it both ways. Not that there's really any reason for us to keep going our way—or so we should have learned. That's why Jesus puts it so bluntly in our text: "Whoever wants to save his life will lose it." In other words, if you want to have things your way—to be in control, to be the captain of your own ship, or to carve out your own destiny—you may set out to save your life, but you'll end up losing it. For doing it our way—walking in the path of self-service, pride, and our own sinful nature—leads nowhere except to death and destruction.

Jesus invites us to do it his way—to take up our crosses and follow him. "Hold on!" our sinful nature cries out. "No cross for me! Crosses hurt. Suffering isn't fun. I don't want to deal with hardship, suffering, and loss. And if following Jesus means walking the road of the cross, count me out. I'd much rather get than give. I'm more interested in pleasure than pain. So the cross is okay for you, Jesus, but not for me."

Now to bear our crosses and follow Jesus may *look* like death, pain, and hardship. But, in reality, it is life in disguise. With eyes of faith, we see beyond the hardship of the cross to the eternal realities, because what you and I call life is actually a living death. The cross is

God's way of freeing us from our prison of sin and giving us a real life to live. We have nothing to lose except our sin and guilt and shame. And we have everything to gain as he continues to strengthen us with his Holy Word and to feed us with the gift of his precious body and blood in his Holy Supper. In bearing our crosses, we lose our lives to sin and receive his life unto eternity.

> **Then let us follow Christ our Lord and take the cross appointed and, firmly clinging to his Word, in suffering be undaunted. For those who bear the battle's strain the crown of heavenly life obtain. Amen.**

The Road of Death

Or don't you know that all of us who were baptized
into Christ Jesus were baptized into his death?
We were therefore buried with him through baptism
into death in order that, just as Christ was raised
from the dead through the glory of the Father,
we too may live a new life.
(Romans 6:3,4)

There may be a few folks by now who have
become a bit weary of all this talk about the cross and
death. To focus in such an unrelenting way on the
cross almost seems a bit depressing after awhile. Yet
focus on the cross we must! For there is a direct link
between the death of Jesus and every one of us. God in
his mercy has provided this link between this space and
time of ours and the historical event of the cross. That
link is called Baptism.

Without that link our Lenten observance would just
be an empty religious exercise, and the death of Jesus
would be simply an object of contemplation. And while
the memory of his sacrifice might warm our hearts

whenever we thought about the cross, in reality it would do nothing for us. All the benefits of his forgiveness and love and life would be merely nice religious ideas. But in Baptism Jesus killed our sinful nature and gave us a new life to live. There he took us in his arms, sins and all, and carried us with him into his tomb where he buried all our sins. That is the reality of Baptism. And so it's an important question the apostle raises in this text: "Don't you know that all of us who were baptized into Christ Jesus were baptized into his death?"

Well, no, to be perfectly honest, we don't all know that, do we? And if we do know it, we forget it frequently. That's why we're so often overtaken by guilt and imprisoned in the bondage of sin. That's why the memory of past sins haunts us, and the burden of our present guilt crushes us. We all have the habit of creeping back into the old prison cells of our favorite sins. We keep thinking we should get a grip on ourselves and change our lives, but we can't.

You can't tame the sinful nature, and you can't reform sin. We'd like to think we can change our own sinful hearts by resolving to clean up our act. But it doesn't work. There's only one cure for sin: death. You can either die alone, or you can die in Jesus.

And so daily our sinful nature needs to die in Jesus. That's exactly what happens when we confess our sins. When we deliberately take our sins out of the secret hiding places of our hearts and execute them by repentance and confession, it is nothing less than a renewal of the death we died in Baptism with Jesus and a new bestowal of the life we received there with him. So Lent is not a time to reminisce over Jesus' death. We have a share in his cross by our baptisms. And his cross of sin and death means life and light for us forever and ever.

All who believe and are baptized shall see the Lord's salvation. Baptized into the death of Christ, they are a new creation. Through Christ's redemption they shall stand among the glorious, heavenly band of every tribe and nation. With one accord, O God, we pray, grant us your Holy Spirit. Help us in our infirmity through Jesus' blood and merit. Grant us to grow in grace each day that by this sacrament we may eternal life inherit. Amen.

The Word of God
The Passion of Our Lord Jesus Christ
Drawn from the Four Gospels
Fifth Sunday in Lent

Jesus Is Crucified

The soldiers now had charge of Jesus. They led him outside the city walls to a place called Golgotha, which means "the skull"—a suitable name for the site where executions were carried out. With Jesus were two criminals who were also to be crucified that day. Each prisoner had to carry the cross on which he would be nailed. But along the way, the cross became too heavy for Jesus, and he could no longer carry it. So the centurion stopped a passerby named Simon, a visitor from Cyrene in North Africa, and forced him to carry the cross the rest of the way.

A large number of people followed along behind Jesus. In the crowd were women who were weeping and wailing because they felt sorry for Jesus. But Jesus turned to them and said, "You women of Jerusalem, do not weep for me; but weep for yourselves and for your children. For the time will come when things will be so bad that people will say, 'Happy are the women who cannot have children and who have no babies to nurse. They are the fortunate ones.' Then men will be so terrified that they will say to the mountains, 'Fall on us!' and to the hills, 'Cover us up!' For if men do these things when the tree is green, what will happen when it is dry?"

When they came to Golgotha, the soldiers offered Jesus a drink of wine with some bitter herbs mixed in it; but when he tasted it, he would not drink it.

It was nine o'clock when the soldiers nailed Jesus to his cross. The two criminals were crucified with him—one on his right, the other on his left. Thus the Scripture was fulfilled that says, "And he was numbered with the transgressors."

Soon after the soldiers had nailed Jesus onto the cross, he prayed, "Father, forgive them, for they do not know what they are doing."

On a board fastened above Jesus' head, Pilate had these words written in Aramaic, Latin, and Greek: JESUS OF NAZARETH, THE KING OF THE JEWS. The board was to tell the people who Jesus was and why he was being killed. Since Golgotha was near Jerusalem, many people came by to read the sign. The chief priests did not like the way Pilate had worded the sign. They said to him, "You should not write 'The king of the Jews,' but that *this man said*, 'I am the king of the Jews.'"

Pilate answered, "What I have written, I have written."

According to Roman custom, the soldiers who took part in a crucifixion received the clothing of those they crucified as part of their pay. So the four soldiers who had crucified Jesus started to divide Jesus' clothes among themselves. They shook dice to see which soldier should get which pieces of clothing (his outer garment, head covering, belt, and sandals). His inner tunic, worn next to the body, did not have a seam in it, but was all one piece. The soldiers saw this was a fine expensive garment and that to divide it would ruin it. So they said, "Let's not tear it into pieces, but throw dice for it to see who'll get it." And that's what they did. By doing so, the soldiers fulfilled these words of Scripture: "They divided my garments among them, and for my clothing they cast lots." After that there was nothing more for the soldiers to do than to keep watch while their prisoners died an agonizing death.

All day long the people who came out to the crucifixion and those who passed by said some mean and nasty things to Jesus. Some shook their heads back and forth and said, "You're the one who was going to destroy the temple and build it in three days. So save yourself! Come down from the cross, if you are the Son of God!"

The chief priests and leaders who had brought about Jesus' death were there and went right on mocking and taunting Jesus. "He saved other people," they said. "But he can't save himself. Let the king of Israel come down now from the cross, and then we'll believe him. He said he trusted in God. Well let God save him now if he is so pleased with him, for he said, 'I am the Son of God.'"

The soldiers also mocked him. They came up to him and offered him a drink of sour wine and said, "Since you are the king of the Jews, save yourself!" Even the criminals who were crucified with him said the same kind of insulting things to him. One of the criminals who hung there with him mocked him: "Aren't you the Christ? Save yourself and us!"

But the other criminal rebuked him. "Don't you have any fear of God," he said, "even now when you are under the same sentence of death? We are punished justly, for we are getting what we deserve for what we have done. But this man hasn't done anything wrong." Then he said, "Jesus, remember me when you come into your kingdom."

Jesus answered him, "I tell you the truth, today you will be with me in paradise."

Beneath Jesus' cross stood his mother, his mother's sister, Mary the wife of Cleopas, Mary Magdalene, and John, one of his disciples. When Jesus saw his mother standing there with John, he said to her, "Behold your son." Then he said to John, "Behold your mother." And from that hour on, John took her into his home and looked after her.

By this time it was noon, and a strange and frightening darkness fell over the whole land for the next three hours. The sun stopped shining. The darkness lasted until three o'clock. During this time Jesus said nothing.

Then about three o'clock Jesus cried out in a loud voice, *"Eloi, Eloi, lama sabachthani?"* which means, "My God, my God, why have you forsaken me?"

When some of the people who were standing there heard this, they said, "He's calling for Elijah."

Jesus knew that by now he had done and suffered everything necessary to set men free from their sins; so in order to make the Scriptures come true, he said, "I thirst." There was a jar of sour wine standing there. One of the soldiers ran immediately to get a sponge. He soaked it in the wine and put it on the end of a stick. Then he held it up to Jesus' mouth to give him a drink.

Others said, "Wait and see if Elijah will come and save him."

When Jesus had drunk some of the sour wine, he shouted, "It is finished." Then he cried out, again with a loud voice, "Father, into your hands I commit my spirit." Then he bowed his head and died.

At that moment the curtain in the temple was torn in two parts, from top to bottom. The earth shook, rocks split apart, graves were opened, and a large number of believers who had died became alive and came out of the graves. Their bodies arose at the moment of Christ's death, and after the Savior's own resurrection, they appeared in the city of Jerusalem.

When the Roman centurion who was in charge of the crucifixion saw the way Jesus died and the miracles that had taken place, he began praising God, saying,

"Surely this was the Son of God and a man who was innocent of any wrong."

The people who had gathered to see Jesus crucified now began to return to Jerusalem. Even as they beat their breasts, they had the feeling that something terribly wrong had happened. And Jesus' friends and the women who had come with him from Galilee stood at a distance and watched everything that happened.

The Burial of Jesus

Jesus died about three o'clock on Friday afternoon. Only a few hours were left until sunset. At sundown the Jewish Sabbath would begin, and this was a great, or special, Sabbath because it was the Sabbath at the beginning of the Passover celebration, which lasted a week.

The Jews did not want the body of Jesus or the bodies of the two criminals left on their crosses any longer than sundown, the start of the Sabbath, which was only about three hours away. So some members of the Sanhedrin hurried to see Pilate. They asked him if the legs of the crucified men could be broken so they would die more quickly and their bodies could be taken away. Pilate's soldiers found the two criminals still alive and broke their legs. But when they examined Jesus they found that he was already dead, so they did not break his legs. But to make sure he was dead, one of the soldiers pierced his side with a spear. When he saw blood and water flow out, he had no doubt that Jesus was dead. In this way two prophecies about Jesus were fulfilled: "Not one of his bones will be broken" and "They will look on the one they have pierced."

Later on towards the end of the afternoon, a man named Joseph of Arimathea arranged for the burial of Jesus. He was a respected member of the Sanhedrin, but he had not voted for Jesus' death as had most of the others. He was a good, upright man who was waiting for the kingdom of God. He was a disciple of Jesus, but he had kept his faith secret, because he was afraid to admit openly that he was a follower of Jesus.

But now Joseph gathered up his courage and went to Pilate and asked him for permission to take the body of Jesus from the cross. Pilate, however, was surprised that Jesus was already dead. So he called the centurion and asked him whether Jesus was already dead. Pilate then quickly gave Joseph permission.

So Joseph went to Golgotha and took the body of Jesus down from the cross. Nicodemus came to help him with the burial. He was the man who had come by night to talk with Jesus. He, like Joseph, had been a secret disciple of Jesus. But now he too was no longer afraid to let people know that he was a friend of Jesus. Nicodemus had brought along no less than one hundred pounds of fine-smelling spices for the burial. Together they took the body of Jesus and wrapped long strips of the linen cloth around it, sprinkling the spices between the layers of cloth. They also wrapped a linen cloth around his head.

Now, Joseph had a new grave, carved out of rock. It was like a cave. He had intended it to be the burial place for his family, but no one had been buried there yet. It was close to the place where Jesus had been crucified, in a park-like grove or garden. And that made it possible for Joseph and Nicodemus to complete their work of burying Jesus before the Sabbath began at sundown.

The women from Galilee followed them from Golgotha and watched everything that was done. They saw where the tomb was and how the two men laid Jesus' body in it. They watched as a large stone was rolled in front of the opening to the grave to close off the entrance.

The Sabbath had now begun. They all left the grave, and the women went home to prepare more spices and perfumes. They wanted to put them on the body of Jesus when they returned on Sunday. They wanted to give him a proper burial since everything had been done in such a hurry.

Even though Jesus was now dead and buried, his enemies were still worried. They remembered that Jesus had prophesied that he would rise again from the dead on the third day. So that evening—which was now Saturday—the chief priests and the Pharisees went to see Pilate. "Sir," they said, "we remember that while he was still alive, that liar said, 'After three days I will come back to life.' So will you give the order to your soldiers to guard the grave until the third day is over? Otherwise his disciples might come and steal his body and then claim that he has risen from the dead. If that should happen, we would be faced with a greater deception than the first one. Then the people would really believe he was the Messiah he claimed to be."

Pilate answered, "Do as you like; take some soldiers with you to guard the tomb. Go and make the tomb as secure as you know how."

So they went to the grave and fixed a seal to the stone that blocked the entrance. No one could tamper with it now without breaking the seals and so being discovered.

Then the Jewish leaders went back to the city and left the Roman soldiers standing guard at the grave.

He Must Be Killed?

He then began to teach them that the Son of Man
must suffer many things and be rejected
by the elders, chief priests and teachers of the law,
and that he must be killed
and after three days rise again.
(Mark 8:31)

The disciples were all excited about this Jesus who gave every indication of being the Messiah. They were happy to be on his team. They were delighted to see the admiring crowds that thronged around him. They were thrilled to see the miracles he performed. They were eager to hear what he taught. That is, they were eager—to a point. But when Jesus began to teach them about the cross, they weren't so excited. "He then began to teach them that the Son of Man must suffer many things and be rejected by the elders, chief priests, and teachers of the law, and that he must be killed and after three days rise again." That kind of talk didn't sit too well with the disciples. In fact, Peter took Jesus aside and began to rebuke him.

Peter wanted to let Jesus know that you just don't get ahead in the world that way. You don't achieve anything through suffering. You don't succeed by rejection. You don't make a name for yourself by being killed. These elders, chief priests, and teachers of the law Jesus was talking about were, after all, not just religious figures. They constituted the Sanhedrin, the highest governing body of the land. To be rejected by these men would mean expulsion from the people of Israel—not just to be a man without a country, but to be a man without a God.

Yet Jesus had a word for Peter about the cross. "No, Peter," he, in effect, was saying, "there's been no mistake in what I've told you. This is exactly the way it has been planned all along." You see, Peter had missed the point. Jesus didn't say, "This is what I *want* to do: to suffer, be rejected, and die." He said, "The Son of Man *must* suffer many things . . . and . . . he *must* be killed and after three days rise again."

There is a divine MUST, you see, that gives meaning to the cross of Jesus. The whole Lenten scene: the agony in the garden, the mob, the betrayal, the kangaroo court trial, the stripping and mocking, the torture and flogging, the nailing of his living flesh to an instrument of death—all of this is NECESSARY in God's game plan.

For way back in Eden, God had warned: in the day you eat of the fruit of the tree of the knowledge of good and evil, YOU WILL SURELY DIE. And we know the sad result of mankind's rebellion. In wanting to be like God, we have become demonic instead. In reaching out to make something of ourselves, we become broken and empty. In striving for life, we brought death down around our ears. And there's no way around it, apart from God. The only way out from under the death sentence in which we all live was for God himself to die. And die he did, taking all our sins with him into his death so that he might give us his life instead—the life that has no end!

> **Thou hast borne the smiting only that my wounds might all be whole. Thou hast suffered, sad and lonely, rest to give my weary soul; yea, the curse of God enduring, blessing unto me securing. Thousand, thousand thanks shall be, dearest Jesus, unto thee. Amen.**

Victory at the Cross

"Now is the time for judgment on this world;
now the prince of this world will be driven out.
But I, when I am lifted up from the earth,
will draw all men to myself."
He said this to show the kind of death
he was going to die.
(John 12:31-33)

We all like victory. We enjoy coming out on top. We're interested in winning friends and influencing people. We like to see nice guys get ahead. We all want to be happy. We all like winners. And Jesus is a winner. Let there be no mistake about that. Jesus brings joy, and Jesus brings victory—it's just that his victory comes in the shape of a cross.

"Unless a kernel of wheat falls to the ground and dies," Jesus said, "it remains only a single seed." Death is what Jesus was talking about. His death. There was only one way for him to defeat this enemy of all enemies and win this battle, only one way to dislodge the prince of this world: *God himself* would have to die.

This was the hour for which he had been sent from the Father's throne, the time of the final assault on the enemy. Victory was at hand. But this victory had a price tag attached. Jesus knew he must be lifted up on his cross. And he said, "Now is my heart troubled." And you would be troubled too if you knew you had to bear the brunt of the wrath of God against the sins of the world. It meant real blood and real pain and real tears. And so in the Garden of Gethsemane, the Son of God lay prostrate in the dirt in fervent prayer that the Father would find some other way to save the world. But the answer he got was, "No." There was no way to win apart from death. There would be no victory for Jesus apart from his cross.

But there's something else we can't miss here. You and I are forever trying to figure out why bad things happen to good people. It's not fair, we're quick to point out. "Fairness has nothing to do with it," says Jesus. Rather, the cross and suffering are God's way of keeping us close to the victory that he has won for us on the cross.

Whoever said it would be easy to be a Christian? Whoever said there would be no ridicule from friends, no subtle pressure at work, no open antagonism from the world? Whoever said the Christian life would be smooth, with no sickness and no blue Mondays or black Fridays, with no stress and no strain in between? Whoever said that Christians would never have sorrow or pain or tears? Certainly not Jesus. "Whoever serves me," he says, "must follow me." His way is the way of the cross.

We need the cross, for we all deserve death. And death is what we got. In Jesus, that is. Baptized into the death and resurrection of Jesus, his death is our death. And his life is our life too—by faith. Victory is sweet. And at his cross, Jesus won the victory for us for all eternity.

We are the Lord's. His all-sufficient merit, sealed on the cross, to us this grace accords. We are the Lord's and all things shall inherit. Whether we live or die, we are the Lord's. We are the Lord's. Then let us gladly tender our souls to him in deeds, not empty words. Let heart and tongue and life combine to render no doubtful witness that we are the Lord's. Amen.

Love So Amazing, So Divine

*From the sixth hour until the ninth hour
darkness came over all the land.
About the ninth hour Jesus cried out in a loud voice,
"Eloi, Eloi lama sabachthani?"—which means,
"My God, my God, why have you forsaken me?"*
(Matthew 27:45,46)

Darkness—the very word conjures up emptiness, abandonment, lifelessness, and loneliness. And so it should. The day Jesus died, there was darkness over all the land from noon until three. There was darkness, and there was death, and there was silence. For God was silent that day. There was no voice from heaven at Calvary. Instead, God the Son called up from earth, "My God, my God, why have you forsaken me?"

Do you know what that's like? Have you ever been forsaken? Have you ever been alone? I mean really alone? Have you ever been left all alone to fend for yourself? I suppose most of us can think of times we were indeed *lonely*. But chances are that we have never really been *alone*—we've just *felt* as if we were. But Jesus didn't just *feel* alone; he *was* alone on his cross, drinking the cup he had been given to drink—the cup of the Father's wrath and punishment, the just penalty for the sins of all the world.

Amazing! Amazing, indeed, that God would come so far and stoop so low as to become one of us and then die the death of a common sinner in darkness, silence, and abandonment—the victim of his Father's wrath. Amazing love it took—amazing and divine. Stripped of all his clothes, he was nailed up in shame and degradation to die a horrible and painful death. That took love surpassing human love.

And that love is yours this day. You may be without a care in the world, or you may be loaded down with worry and despair. You may have the compassion and understanding of your friends, or it may seem to you that you're all alone, without a friend in this world. But no matter. Whoever you are and whatever your situation, there is love for you this day. There is One who knows your heart, one who shares your joy and knows your pain. There is One who bears your sorrows and carries all your grief in his own mind and heart. There is One who understands better and more fully than you yourself do just what lies heaviest on your mind and deepest in your soul. He wraps himself in Word and water, bread and wine to comfort you with his presence, to enfold you in his forgiveness, love, and peace.

That One is none other than Jesus Christ. And because of him and what he has done, you are not alone.

132

He entered into darkness and death that you might have his very life and light. He died forsaken, abandoned, and alone so that you need never be alone again—not now, not ever. So take heart! For there is light and love and life for you this day and even forevermore.

When I survey the wondrous cross on which the Prince of glory died, my richest gain I count but loss and pour contempt on all my pride. Were the whole realm of nature mine, that were a tribute far too small. Love so amazing, so divine, demands my soul, my life, my all. Amen.

Getting Rid of Guilt

*Then Peter remembered the word the Lord
had spoken to him: "Before the rooster crows today,
you will disown me three times."
And he went outside and wept bitterly.*
(Luke 22:61,62)

"And he went outside and wept bitterly." Those were no "crocodile tears" Peter cried. Those were the tears of a broken man—tears of remorse and shame.

That same Peter had been the first one to confess Jesus as the Son of the living God. In fact, that's how he had gotten his name. For that confession Jesus had given him the name Peter, which means "the rock." And a rock he had been. In Gethsemane he was the disciple who drew his sword to defend Jesus from capture by his enemies. "Though they all fall away because of you," Peter had boldly promised Jesus, "I will never deny you." And for that moment at least, he had been ready to back his words with his actions.

But just a few hours later, Peter's bold claim crumbled. In the gray light of early dawn, Peter stood in the high priest's courtyard and, with cursing and with swearing, denied not only that he was a disciple, but that he had ever known Jesus. And just then the rooster crowed. Jesus turned and looked at Peter. And Peter remembered the words of Jesus: "Before the rooster crows today, you will disown me three times." And there in the night, this giant of faith, this great big rock of a man, broke down into tears.

Our interest in Peter is not merely historical. It is no casual curiosity that brings us to examine these events. For you and I *are like* Peter. We too have denied our Lord. Time and again we have turned our backs on him, and by our words and by our actions, we have denied ever knowing him. We *are* Peter. His need is our need. Therefore we come in this holy season of Lent for repentance. We come, in other words, for a change—a change so deep and so profound, a change so very real, it can only be called a new creation. We pray with the psalmist: "Create in me a clean heart, O God, and renew a right spirit within me" (Psalm 51:10).

You see, if we claim that we have no sin, we deceive ourselves, and the truth is not in us. But if we confess our sins, God, who is faithful and just, will forgive our sins and cleanse us from all unrighteousness. That's confession and absolution in action: a simple matter of truth. Telling the truth to God, we admit the bitter, awful truth of our sin. Hearing the truth from God, we learn that, as far as the east is from the west, so far has he removed our sins from us. He placed them all on

Jesus, who bore our sins with him into death, that he might absolve—that is, cleanse and forgive—everyone who trusts in him.

That's how we deal with guilt: the bitterness of sins confessed and the sweet truth of sins absolved and gone forever in Jesus' name. He places his forgiveness into the preaching of the gospel, into Holy Baptism, into the Lord's Supper, and into holy absolution. He takes our guilt and gives us his forgiveness, life, and salvation. And by grace through faith, we receive the peace of mind and heart that is the joy and peace of Christ himself!

Lord, we confess our numerous faults, how great our guilt has been, how vain and foolish all our thoughts, how deeply stained with sin. 'Tis from the mercy of our God that all our hopes begin. 'Tis by the water and the blood our souls are washed from sin. Amen.

On Cross Bearing

After they had mocked him, they took off the robe
and put his own clothes on him.
Then they led him away to crucify him.
As they were going out,
they met a man from Cyrene, named Simon,
and they forced him to carry the cross.
(Matthew 27:31,32)

We all love a parade. We can picture it in our mind's eye: Jesus on his donkey, the palms waving, the crowds cheering, and little children singing, "Hosanna!" But Palm Sunday leads to Good Friday. And Holy Week helps us remember that the only way to glory is through the cross; the only way to victory is through affliction; the only way to life is through death.

So let's turn our attention to another parade, the one that came towards the end of Holy Week: the Good Friday parade, when the soldiers led Jesus out to Golgotha. Very little about that procession is recorded except the curious detail that they met Simon of Cyrene on their way out and that the Roman soldiers forced him to carry the cross for Jesus. Whatever the reason, this man Simon was the one picked to bear the cross of Jesus. And he is not alone. We all have our crosses to bear as well.

Can it really be so? Can it be possible that the God who loves us with an everlasting love could take away our security, our health, our loved ones—and still be a God of love? It is possible that he may lay a cross on our backs, like the cross that was placed on Simon's back? Can't we just go merrily on, mouthing our pious platitudes and pretending life is grand?

Well, of course, we can't. But we don't need to. And that's just the point. We know that God is at his best when life is at its worst. Our hope is not built upon our job security, our health and welfare, our physical comfort, or our income. All is not right with the world just because God is in his heaven. No, all is right with the world because God was on the cross—because God himself died on that cross on Calvary, paying the penalty for all of our sin and rebellion.

Holy Week keeps us honest. We don't have to pretend that everything is just peachy. It isn't. But nobody—least of all God—promised you a rose garden. He has not promised that you will be healthy, wealthy, and wise. But he has promised that there will be strength for every weakness, hope for every heartache, peace in all turmoil, and consolation in every pain. For Jesus has already been stricken, smitten, and afflicted so that we might find health, healing, and comfort in his holy wounds.

Simon had his cross that day, and we will have ours as well—a burden, a hardship, an affliction: each especially designed to drive us to repentance, to draw us to our Father's arms, where we find shelter and peace. The One who shared his cross with Simon will share your cross with you. For Jesus Christ is with you in your cross, whatever it may be. And with his body broken and blood outpoured, we find forgiveness for all our sins, life in all its fullness, and eternal salvation.

Defend us, Lord, from sin and shame; help us by your almighty name to bear our crosses patiently, consoled by your great agony. For thus the certainty we gain that you will always true remain and not forsake us in our strife but lead us out of death to life. Amen.

The King Approaches

Rejoice greatly, O Daughter of Zion!
Shout, Daughter of Jerusalem!
See, your king comes to you,
righteous and having salvation,
gentle and riding on a donkey,
on a colt, the foal of a donkey.
(Zechariah 9:9)

The magnificent events we review as we move towards Holy Week are no myth, no parable, no made-for-TV movie. It was in real life and in real history that Jesus was crucified, died, was buried, and, on the third day, rose again from the dead. And we will, by the grace of God, meditate upon the miracle of all of that in the next days.

Now it all seems like ancient history to us. But when our text was first written, Palm Sunday still lay hundreds of years in the future. The prophet Zechariah, inspired by the Holy Spirit, looks ahead down the corridor of time and describes for us what he sees: the entrance of Christ into Jerusalem. The description is that of a royal wedding; the language he uses is that of betrothal. God's people, Israel, is the bride, and the Lord, the God of Israel, is the husband who comes in regal procession to meet his bride. Yes, he is "righteous and having salvation." But he comes "gentle and riding on a donkey, on a colt, the foal of a donkey."

The prophecy of Zechariah had its fulfillment in Jesus' entrance into Jerusalem on that day we celebrate as Palm Sunday. So on the very brink of Holy Week, you and I are brought once more face-to-face with Jesus. He has both a warning and a promise for us. The warning is clear: "Not everyone who says to me 'Lord, Lord,' will enter the kingdom of heaven, but only he who does the will of my Father who is in heaven" (Matthew 7:21). Yet there is also this clear promise: "My Father's will is that everyone who looks to the Son and believes in him shall have eternal life, and I will raise him up at the last day" (John 6:40). That promise, his promise, comes to us from the very mouth of Jesus.

What better time for you and me to prepare for Holy Week by heeding his word of warning and his word of promise? What better time to be present in the Lord's house—to trace his steps from the upper room where he took the bread and wine of the Passover and gave us his Holy Supper, giving us to eat of his body and drink of his blood. Then we journey on with him to Calvary, where he gave the last full measure of his devotion, laying down his life for us all—only to take it up again in his glorious rising to life again on Easter Day.

Even as we sing our hosannas, our Father opens up his arms to proclaim his love once more. For each and every tarnished sinner, the Son has shed his blood and comes to us each Lord's Day, disguised in the lowly garb of his precious Word and Holy Sacrament, as the bridegroom of his church to claim his bride—that's you and me, by the grace of God—unblemished, pure, and undefiled in his redeeming love.

All glory, laud, and honor to you, Redeemer, King, to whom the lips of children made sweet hosannas ring. You are the King of Israel and David's royal Son, now in the Lord's name coming, our King and blessed one. Amen.

The Word of God

For Palm Sunday
Readings and Prayers

In Preparation for Holy Week

Psalm 24

The earth is the LORD's, and everything in it,
    the world and all who live in it;
for he founded it upon the seas
    and established it upon the waters.
Who may ascend the hill of the LORD?
    Who may stand in his holy place?
He who has clean hands and a pure heart,
    who does not lift up his soul to an idol
    or swear by what is false.
He will receive blessing from the LORD
    and vindication from God his Savior.
Such is the generation of those who seek him,
    who seek your face, O God of Jacob.

Lift up your heads, O you gates;
    be lifted up, you ancient doors,
    that the King of glory may come in.

Who is this King of glory?
> The LORD strong and mighty,
> the LORD mighty in battle.
Lift up your heads, O you gates;
> lift them up, you ancient doors,
> that the King of glory may come in.
Who is he, this King of glory?
> The LORD almighty—
> he is the King of glory.

Prayer

Lord Jesus, on this Palm Sunday, let our minds dwell on your glory as it lit up the lives of all who came in contact with you. We confess you as our Lord, our Savior, and our King. Inspire us to bring the news of your salvation to all people, that every knee may bow before you and every tongue confess that you are indeed the Lord of glory who hath bought us.

The Gospel of John 12:12-16

The next day the great crowd that had come for the Feast heard that Jesus was on his way to Jerusalem. They took palm branches and went out to meet him, shouting,
> "Hosanna!"
> "Blessed is he who comes in the name of the Lord!"
> "Blessed is the King of Israel!"

Jesus found a young donkey and sat upon it, as it is written,

"Do not be afraid, O Daughter of Zion; see, your king is coming, seated on a donkey's colt."

At first his disciples did not understand all this. Only after Jesus was glorified did they realize that these things had been written about him and that they had done these things to him.

Confession of Sin

O almighty God, merciful Father, I, a poor, miserable sinner, confess unto thee all my sins and iniquities with which I have ever offended thee and justly deserved thy temporal and eternal punishment. But I am heartily sorry for them and sincerely repent of them, and I pray thee of thy boundless mercy and for the sake of the holy, innocent, bitter sufferings and death of thy beloved Son, Jesus Christ, to be gracious and merciful to me, a poor, sinful being.

God's Promise

If we claim to be without sin, we deceive ourselves and the truth is not in us. If we confess our sins, he is faithful and just and will forgive us our sins and purify us from all unrighteousness. (1 John 1:8,9)

The Lord's Prayer

Our Father, who art in heaven,
    Hallowed be thy name,
    thy kingdom come,
    thy will be done
        on earth as it is in heaven.
Give us this day our daily bread;
and forgive us our trespasses,
    as we forgive those
    who trespass against us;
and lead us not into temptation,
but deliver us from evil.
For thine is the kingdom
    and the power and the glory
    forever and ever. Amen.

"The hour has come for the Son of Man to be glorified."
(John 12:23)

Why, God, Why?

My God, my God, why have you forsaken me?
Why are you so far from saving me,
so far from the words of my groaning?
(Psalm 22:1)

Is there anyone with a heart so hard as to not be moved by Jesus' desolate cry: "My God, my God, why have you forsaken me?" Is there anyone who doesn't know what it's like to be abandoned or forsaken? Probably not. But the issue goes deeper than that. Is there anyone who knows what it's like to cry out to God in desperation and get no response? To be at the end of your rope and to pray and pray and pray and be met with nothing but silence?

Perhaps you've known that kind of despair, perhaps not. Perhaps you've *felt* alone, *felt* totally abandoned. Our Lord Jesus *was* actually alone on his cross. He was abandoned by the Father. He was forsaken in death. You can hear the biting pain in his heart-wrenching prayer: "My God, my God, why?"

Thousands of years before, Abraham had stretched out his hand to slay his son, Isaac. But the angel of the Lord had intervened. At Calvary that shocking scene was reenacted. But this time there was no last minute intervention. Isaac was spared. Jesus was not. He died. It was a real death. It could be no other way. Because, you see, the Lord laid on him the iniquity of us all. God made him to be sin for us, and the sinner must die. The righteous wrath of the Father would not allow sin to go without penalty. The scales of divine justice had to be balanced. If hell is absolute separation from God, then this was a hell of a death to die. For in his death, God the Son was abandoned and forsaken by God the Father.

The solemn rites we observe during this Lenten season are the church's way of impressing on all the faithful that our Lord Jesus was indeed bruised for our iniquities, that he was wounded for our transgressions, that with his stripes we are healed—that he is the very Lamb of God who takes away the sin of the world.

In Jesus' degradation and in his dying, he teaches us all a lesson: a lesson that may be, in fact, the most important key to life in this world and the certain key to life in the world to come. The lesson? That strength is found in weakness, that joy is found in sorrow, and that life is found in death.

The cross is the very pattern for our life and the fiber of our existence. When we daily die to sin, we daily rise to righteousness—we rise to live again with Jesus. And so Jesus bids us come and follow him. We believe his promise, and so we rise and follow after, not knowing where we go, but only that his hand is leading us and his love is supporting us.

Let us also die with Jesus. His death from the second death, from our soul's destruction, frees us, quickens us with life's glad breath. Let us mortify, while living, flesh and blood and die to sin. And the grave that shuts us in shall but prove the gate to heaven. Jesus, here I die to thee, there to live eternally. Amen.

The Kingdom, the Power, and the Glory

Then he [the criminal] said, "Jesus, remember me
when you come into your kingdom."
Jesus answered him, "I tell you the truth,
today you will be with me in paradise."
(Luke 23:42,43)

One of the central truths of Christian living is that you can see more by faith than you can by sight. The dying thief on Calvary saw one thing with his eyes but quite another by faith. What was visible to his eyes that day at Calvary was a painful execution. Nevertheless, he turned to Jesus, already in the grip of death, and said, "Jesus, remember me when you come into your kingdom." Jesus certainly didn't look like a king. He looked like a bleeding man, a dying victim. But the thief addressed him like a victorious hero.

Now, that's faith. And that's precisely what you and I need most of all in this world. We certainly thank our gracious God for our eyes and ears, our reason, and all our senses. But, important as these are, faith is still the greater gift. For faith alone sees the hidden realities. Faith alone looks ahead to all eternity. And faith alone is able to confess that the sufferings of this present time are not worth comparing to the glories that will be revealed in us. Faith alone sees that there will be peace at the last.

Unfortunately, however, we rarely have the faith of the dying thief. We keep thinking that the power and glory of God are like the power and glory of this world. We keep looking for God to bowl us over with his presence, to show us his power by abolishing the problems in our lives, to reveal his glory to us by making us glorious. We learn in this text, though, that God's power is made perfect in weakness and his glory is revealed in the midst of shame. The dying thief looked at the naked, bleeding man hanging beside him and called him king.

That day on the cross, heaven intersected with earth. That day eternity broke into time. That day in the very midst of death, there was life. The thief saw beyond pain and death and looked clearly into the reality of the kingdom of God. And that thief has nothing over us. The kingdom of God is here too in our very midst. The kingdom, the power, and the glory are hidden under the washing, Word, and meal Jesus gave us.

It's the same for us as it was at Calvary, you see. It's no different for those of us who have the Word and the Sacrament of Christ than it was for the thief who hung next to the cross of Christ. Here the Lamb of God, who takes away the sin of the world, takes away our sin and brings life and immortality to light. Here, in the name of Jesus Christ and by his authority, sins are forgiven and life is restored. Here broken hearts are mended. Here, in the presence of the King, we find healing and peace once more. Christ, our King, guards and keeps us always in his presence. The kingdom is here, you see— and with the kingdom of God comes the power of God and the glory of God, both now and forevermore.

> **My faith looks up to thee, thou Lamb of Calvary, Savior divine. Now hear me while I pray. Take all my guilt away. Oh, let me, from this day, be wholly thine! Amen.**

My Soul, My Life, My All

When the centurion and those who were with him,
keeping watch over Jesus,
saw the earthquake and what took place,
they were filled with awe, and said,
"Truly this was the Son of God!"
(Matthew 27:54 RSV)

Of all the characters of the passion history who stood around the cross of Christ, the centurion is the one we need most to hear. He has the last word at the cross. And what a word it is: "Truly this was the Son of God!" Some, that day, wept at the cross. Others scoffed or hurled insults and mockery at Jesus. But the centurion confessed his faith, his faith that Jesus was the Son of God. This was not merely the centurion's faith. It is our faith too. This is the faith in which we live. And, by the grace of God, it will be the faith in which we die. In fact, this is the faith that will enable us to stand pure and undefiled before the judgment seat of God on the Last Day. Therefore, this is our unswerving confession: Jesus Christ is Lord and God.

The centurion was overwhelmed by all he saw and heard in the cosmic darkness of that day. First our Savior's dying words, his head bowed down in death. Then the shaking of the earth itself, the tearing of the temple curtain, the splitting of the rocks, the rending of the tombs, and the resurrection of the dead. It was a mini judgment day.

The centurion confessed with his lips what he believed in his heart: "Truly this was the Son of God!" So said the centurion; so say we. No shaking earth, no rending tombs surround us. But the same Lord who was crucified there that day, who died and was buried, who rose again on the third day, who ascended into heaven, and who now sits at the right hand of the Father—this same Lord Jesus calls forth our prayers and praises.

We too confess with our mouths what we believe in our hearts. And in our hearts we know that there's more to the cross than meets the eye. In our hearts we know that Jesus was put to death for our transgressions and raised again for our justification. In our hearts we know that it was for us and for our salvation that Jesus Christ was made man and suffered all the pains of the cross, making himself to be the atoning sacrifice for our sins.

Meanwhile, the world around us goes blindly on, paying little attention to this holy Lenten season. And many of us have all we can do just to keep on keeping on. Yet, the centurion's confession lifts us above all of that. We are lifted above whatever weighs upon our hearts and minds to fix our eyes on something that transcends us all. In this Lenten season, we choose to focus on the cross of Christ, to learn again what it means to have a Savior and a Lord. We learn again that, in the wondrous cross of Christ, there is, for every penitent sinner, pardon, forgiveness, and remission from each and every sin. Truly this is the Son of God!

> Thou hast suffered great affliction and hast borne it patiently, even death by crucifixion, fully to atone for me. Thou didst choose to be tormented that my doom should be prevented. Thousand, thousand thanks shall be, dearest Jesus, unto thee. Amen.

A Feast of Deliverance
Maundy Thursday

"And when your children say to you,
'What do you mean by this service?'
you shall say, 'It is the sacrifice of the LORD's *passover,*
for he passed over the houses of the people of Israel in Egypt,
when he slew the Egyptians but spared our houses.'"
And the people bowed their heads and worshiped.
(Exodus 12:26,27 RSV)

On Maundy Thursday, realizing we are never too old or too wise to learn afresh, we pause from the frenzy of our hurried lives to ask, "What do we mean by this service?" On the night in which he was betrayed, our Lord sat at table in an upper room to give a new testament in his blood, the deliverance from bondage to sin and death. The night he gave us his Holy Supper, Jesus said, "Do this in remembrance of me." What did Jesus mean by this service?

In order to answer that question, we must turn the clock back thousands of years to another night, long before the night of Jesus' betrayal. We must return to the dark and scary night that marked the end of slavery in Egypt for God's people, the Israelites. It was the night of Passover, the night God dramatically rescued his chosen people. That night God set his captive people free. He forced the hand of an obstinate Pharaoh by unleashing his wrath on the whole land of Egypt. God's destroying angel went through all the land, killing the firstborn offspring of man and beast. Death visited every household, except where blood marked the door.

The blood of a sacrificial lamb, smeared on the doorpost of the household, and its body consumed in a ritual meal of deliverance, was God's antidote to death for the people of Israel. The blood was a sign, a remembrance, both for the people in that house and for God himself. That sign indicated that God in his mercy would spare that household from sure and certain death. "When I see the *blood*," God declared, "I will pass over you, and no plague shall fall upon you to destroy you."

As the blood of the Passover lamb delivered the people of Israel from sure and certain death, so the blood of Jesus Christ our Savior delivers us from the wrath of God and cleanses us from all sin. As the Israelites were given the body of that lamb to eat in solemn joy in that Passover meal, we too are given to eat of the sacrifice by which we are delivered from death and hell and given life eternal. For under the bread of the Holy Supper, our Lord Jesus gives us to eat of his very body, and the wine is the very blood he shed for the remission of all our sins, given to drink as a source of renewal, cleansing, and everlasting life for all who trust in him.

What do we mean by this service? Without the shedding of blood, there is no forgiveness of sins. Giving his body over into death, our Lord Jesus is the antidote to our death and the source of our Life. He promises that whoever eats his flesh and drinks his blood abides in him and he in them, and they have his LIFE alive in them. We kneel in holy awe with reverent faith and joy to receive the feast prepared for us. This is the night of our deliverance.

Lord Jesus Christ, you have prepared this feast for our salvation. It is your body and your blood, and at your invitation as weary souls, with sin oppressed, we come to you for needed rest, for comfort, and for pardon. Amen.

The Devil Defeated
Good Friday

When he had received the drink,
Jesus said, "It is finished."
With that, he bowed his head and gave up his spirit.
(John 19:30)

Today we celebrate Satan's defeat. It was achieved by our Lord Jesus—who by his cross and death has triumphed over the devil. As Satan once deceived Adam and Eve by a tree in the garden, so now Satan has been overcome on the tree of the cross. The very source of death has become the source of life for us all. All of this and more, Jesus clearly proclaims in his last triumphant cry: "It is finished."

"Great!" we say to ourselves. "Now we can relax and get on with life." Lent is kind of a drag, and it's nice to have all of this behind us so we can get back to business as usual.

But you can't walk away from the words of Jesus, and you can't escape the cross. For his words and his cross are for you. "It is finished," Jesus said. And having said this, he died. He died a very real death. And this is the most important reality in all the world. Just because you and I know that Jesus came back from the dead, we tend to skirt this issue, skipping over the death of Jesus as an unfortunate mistake. But this was no mistake. It was the expressed will and purpose of God the Father to put him forward as the very Lamb of God, who takes away the sin of the world. And there's only one way that could happen: Jesus had to die. Jesus Christ, the Lord of life, died.

When they pierced his side that day, Jesus was dead. Out came blood and water. These are the signs and seals of his death. But that water and blood are also the signs and seals of our redemption. For being baptized with water in the name of the Father and of the Son and of the Holy Spirit, we are baptized into the death of Christ and into his resurrection. Eating his body and drinking his holy, precious blood, we have all the treasures and gifts Jesus earned in that body and blood of his, once given and shed for us for the forgiveness of sins.

How do we know all this? Because Jesus said so. With his dying breath, he cried out, "It is finished." Now is banished sin, death, and hell. So we don't turn away, then, from this Good Friday reality. We are not afraid to face the truth. By this truth we are saved. We do not flinch or shrink from the full depth of the meaning of this day. Because Christ was abandoned by the Father in his death, we will never, ever, be alone—he is always at our side in life. And our confidence on that day in which we die will be the same confidence in

which we live all life long: Jesus Christ and him crucified. "It is finished," he said. That's what he said and
that's what he meant. We can take him at his Word and
cling to his promise: "Whoever eats my flesh and drinks
my blood has eternal life, and I will raise him up at the
last day" (John 6:54).

> Calvary's mournful mountain climb; there, ador-
> ing at his feet, mark that miracle of time, God's
> own sacrifice complete. "It is finished!" hear
> him cry; learn of Jesus Christ to die. Amen.

Baptism Now Saves You

Easter Eve Vigil

> *In this ark a few, that is, eight persons,*
> *were saved by water. In the same way also,*
> *baptism now saves us.*
> (1 Peter 3:20,21 NET)

We stand on holy ground. We stand between death and life, between the font and the altar, between the darkness of Christ's death and the light of Christ's resurrection. On this most holy night, we keep an Easter vigil. This is the night before Christ the life arose from the death. The seal of the grave was about to be broken, and the morning of the new creation was about to break forth.

This is a time to reflect upon the paschal life—the life of the living Lord Jesus Christ, a life so real you can eat it in his Holy Supper, a life so real you can bathe in it in his bath of regeneration and renewal in the Holy Spirit, which we call Baptism. This Baptism, Saint Peter reminds us, "now saves you." It works forgiveness of sins, delivers from death and the devil, and gives eternal salvation to all who believe. It is the strong Word of God in and with the water that does these things, along with faith that trusts this Word of God in the water.

As it was in the beginning, so it is now. As God once created life out of nothing by the sheer power of his Word, so in Holy Baptism he re-creates us in his own image by the power of that same Word. The very same water of Noah's flood, which destroyed the sinful world, was the vehicle of salvation for Noah and his family. That death-dealing and yet life-giving water of the flood in Noah's time foreshadows Baptism. Saint Peter reminds us that in our baptisms, you and I were linked to both death and life: the death and life of Christ.

In Holy Baptism there is a death and resurrection for every believer. That is why Baptism now saves you. Not because water was poured on you, but because by the sheer power of the Word of God, you were put to death and raised to life again. Holy Baptism is our new beginning in the new creation. He who believes and is baptized shall be saved. And if that's you, no matter who you are or where you've been or what you've done, you're free. You're free to live in him.

In the washing of Baptism, we have a real peace. It's the peace purchased on Good Friday with the blood of Jesus for the sins of the world—backed up by his glorious Easter resurrection. And this peace, the Bible tells us, the world cannot give. This peace is present in good times and bad, in thick and thin, in sorrow as well as in joy. This is a peace that comforts even when our conscience accuses us—even in anxiety and in fear. This is a peace solid enough to withstand the worst the world has to offer. In the washing of his baptism, in the eating of his Holy Supper, and in the hearing of his holy gospel he distributes his peace to each of us, giving us forgiveness of sins, life, and salvation. And this peace is yours, even now as we await the triumphant celebrations that come with Easter's dawning light.

> **Now my life is new and holy; I am baptized into Christ. Clothed in him, he lives within me, and I am alive in him. For the sin and death I carried now within his grave lie buried; since by grace I'm dead to sin, now by grace I live in him. Amen.**
>
> —*Harold L. Senkbeil*

Where Is Jesus?
The Resurrection of Our Lord—Easter Day

"Do not be amazed; you seek Jesus of Nazareth,
who was crucified. He has risen, he is not here;
see the place where they laid him."
(Mark 16:6 RSV)

"He is not here." These words turned the world upside down and changed the course of history. Having gone to the tomb to embalm a dead body, the women were astounded to find the stone rolled away. And they were flabbergasted to meet an angel inside the tomb— an angel who greeted them with the astonishing word that Jesus had risen from the dead. This is where Easter begins, with the great proclamation that Jesus Christ has burst the bonds of death and emerged victorious over the grave. "He is not here."

This is the solid foundation on which our faith is built. But if that were all there was to Easter, we needn't bother singing alleluias on this or any day. If all we had of Easter were an empty tomb and an angel, that would be unusual and amazing, but it would mean nothing for our life and for our salvation. An empty tomb without

Jesus does us no good. He's the One we need—the living Lord himself. The real issue for you and me is the same as it was for the women who went to the tomb that first Easter morning: we need to find Jesus.

We need Jesus himself. And three days after he was buried, he appeared in his risen flesh to his disciples that first Easter evening. "Touch me and see," Jesus said. "A ghost does not have flesh and bones, as you see I have." This is the Jesus we need: the flesh and blood Jesus. The Jesus you can hear and touch. And that's exactly the Jesus we have among us, still today. The same Jesus who showed his hands and side to his disciples grants us his joy in his risen flesh—for under the bread and wine of his Holy Supper, he gives us his very body to eat and his blood to drink. The same Jesus who said, "The words I have spoken to you are Spirit and they are life" (John 6:63), still sends forth his servants to preach his words in his name among us—and those words are vibrant and life-giving. They are filled to the brim with his life.

And it is the life of Jesus Christ that we need still today. For it's time to face the truth. It's time to hold up a mirror to our sadly twisted world and see it for what it has become. And as the world becomes more and more chaotic, we have our own share of personal confusion and pain. We have turned our backs on our Creator. We have grieved our God and hurt our neighbors. The sad truth is that sin is not just to be found in the world out there; it lies within our hearts too.

But amid the emptiness and confusion of our world and in the very face of our sin and death comes this glorious Easter gospel: Jesus Christ, the Son of God, was crucified for our offenses and raised again for our justification. And he is here among us. The risen Lord Jesus comes among us yet today, hidden in the water of Baptism, the bread and wine of his Holy Supper, and in the Word proclaimed in his holy name. Where is Jesus? He is here among us! And his gifts remain forever sure: the communion of saints, the forgiveness of sins, the resurrection of the body, and the life everlasting.

Jesus lives! I know full well nothing me from him shall sever, life nor death nor powers of hell part me now from Christ forever. God will be a sure defense; this shall be my confidence. Amen.

Now, "May the God of peace,

who through the blood of the eternal covenant

brought back from the dead our Lord Jesus,

that great Shepherd of the sheep,

equip you with everything good for doing his will,

and may he work in us what is pleasing to him,

through Jesus Christ,

to whom be glory for ever and ever. Amen."

Hebrews 13:20,21

Index to Scripture References

Notes

"The Passion Drawn from the Four Gospels" is an adaptation by the editor of a translation and paraphrase by Werner Franzmann.

The prayers found in the Palm Sunday devotion are from *Meditations* (Vol. 16, No. 1, Northwestern Publishing House) and *The Lutheran Hymnal*.

Except where noted, the prayers in the other devotions are adapted hymn stanzas from *Christian Worship: A Lutheran Hymnal*.